# IT'S NOT BUSINESS, IT'S *Personal*

### The Power of a Relational Church

ROB COLÓN

**It's Not Business, It's Personal:**
**The Power of a Relational Church**

Published by Emberwire Publishing
Orlando, Florida

Copyright © 2025 by Robert Colón

All rights reserved. Except for brief excerpts for review purposes, no part of this book may be reproduced or used in any form without written permission from the publisher.

ISBN: 979-8-9987333-0-7

Cover Design: Katarina Naskovski
Editing: Valerie Jones
Formatting: Dawn Black

Scripture quotations, unless otherwise noted, are taken from the Holy Bible, New International Version®, NIV®.
Copyright © 1973, 1978, 1984, 2011 by Biblica, Inc.™
Used by permission. All rights reserved worldwide.

This book is a work of nonfiction. The views expressed are those of the author and do not necessarily reflect the views of any organizations or individuals mentioned. The information provided is for general guidance and inspiration. Readers are encouraged to consult appropriate professionals for advice related to specific situations.

First Edition 2025
12345678910
Printed in the United States of America

# Table Of Contents

**Dedication** .................................................................... 5

**Acknowledgments** ..................................................... 7

**Foreword** ...................................................................... 9

**Preface** ........................................................................ 11

**Introduction** ............................................................... 15

**Chapter 1** The Foundation of a Relational Church ......... 21

**Chapter 2** Beyond Performance and Rituals ................. 37

**Chapter 3** Moving Beyond Self-Centeredness ............... 53

**Chapter 4** The Ministry of Presence ................................ 73

**Chapter 5** Breaking Barriers to Connection ................... 89

**Chapter 6** Transformation Through Relationship .......... 111

**Chapter 7** Prioritizing Relational Leadership ................ 133

**Chapter 8** Redefining Success ........................................ 155

**Chapter 9** Sustaining Relational Church Culture............173

**Chapter 10** Community Beyond the Four Walls............197

**Conclusion**..................................................................215

**Epilogue A Vision for the Future** ....................................225

**Sources & Biblical References**........................................227

**Acknowledgment Of Influence** ......................................247

# Dedication

*To my father, **Robert Luis**, who left this earth way too early.
If you could see me now, I know you'd be proud.*

*To my grandparents, **Hector** and **Celeste**—
always the voice of reason in my life and my spiritual north.
You showed me what it truly means to live the gospel,
not just in words, but in the way you loved and related to others;
I learned from the best.*

# Acknowledgments

There's no way this book could exist without a whole community of love and support behind it. First, to my incredible wife, Kayla, thank you for being my rock, my biggest cheerleader, and the one who reminds me every day why this work matters. To my children, Gigi, Gia, Xabi, Braelyn, and Elena; your love gives me purpose and a constant reminder of God's goodness. Mom, your spiritual guidance and friendship have shaped who I am. I'm so grateful for your wisdom and prayers through every season.

To my family and friends, thank you for standing by me, lifting me up, and believing in this message from day one. To my pastor, Dr. Agustin Lopez, I can't thank you enough for your mentorship and the way you constantly encourage me to chase after my God-given dreams and calling.

And above all, I give thanks to God: The One who carried me through my toughest moments, never left my side, and truly has been a father to the fatherless and my anchor in every storm. Everything I am and everything I do is grounded in His love and faithfulness.

James 1:27 says, *"Religion that God our Father accepts as pure and faultless is this: to look after orphans and widows in their distress and to keep oneself from being polluted by the world."* That verse is the heartbeat behind this book and, honestly, my entire life.

Thank you to every one of you for being part of this journey.

# Foreword

We find ourselves in a time where institutions and systems have often overshadowed what matters most: real, authentic relationships. Even in the church, the drive for efficiency and polished programs can sometimes take the place of genuine connection. Too often, we see churches operating more like businesses than living communities shaped by the heart of God.

That's why *It's Not Business, It's Personal: The Power of a Relational Church* is such a timely book. This isn't another manual on church growth or organizational strategy. It's an open invitation to rediscover the heartbeat of the Gospel—relationships. Jesus came not to build an organization, but to restore what was broken between us and God, and with one another. This is why the symbolism of the cross can't be missed. Its vertical aspect represents the eternal, divine connection, while the horizontal points to our connection with others. His ministry was profoundly relational. He walked with His people, wept with them, taught them, corrected them, embraced them, and loved them to the end.

As you journey through these pages, you will explore how the Church can recover its essence: to be a living community where love is not a motto, but a practice, where the connection between people matters more than the perfection of a program, where growth is not measured only in numbers, but in the transformation of lives.

Knowing Robert Colon personally, I can say this book was born from pain, observation, and unwavering hope. From the pain of seeing churches operate like businesses. From watching believers become consumers. But also, from the hope that there is still time to return to God's original design: a relational church, where every story is valued, every wound is met with compassion, and every person finds a home and is invited to find their place at the table.

If you've ever felt something is missing from the way we do church, sensed that it was meant to be more than just attendance or activity, and longed for a faith community where you're truly known, loved, and challenged to grow, then this book is for you. Because in God's Kingdom, what matters most isn't business as usual. It's personal.

Robert is someone I've known for most of my life. It's been a journey that has given me a front-row seat to his heart and calling. His passion for a genuine church, centered on relationships and committed to the heart of the Gospel, is evident in all 10 chapters. It is an honor to see how God has formed in him a message so necessary for the Church today.

Robert, thank you for living out this message and for inviting us all to return to the heart of what it means to be the Church. It's an honor to walk this journey with you.

*Dr. Agustin Lopez*
*Founder & Senior Pastor, Misión La Cosecha Church*

# Preface

It all started with my co-worker, Stacey. She had been with the company for over twenty years, putting her heart into everything she did. Stacey wasn't just a co-worker; she was the glue that held everything together. If you had a problem, she was the one to call. If things got chaotic, she was the steady hand that kept it all from falling apart.

So, when she got that call from her doctor, none of us saw it coming. A routine check-up turned into the kind of news that changes everything—cancer. It was the kind of diagnosis that could break anyone. But Stacey? She wasn't about to let it define her. Just like always, she faced it head-on, with the same strength, grace, and determination that made everyone admire her in the first place.

Stacey wasn't just a hard worker, she was unstoppable. Over the years, she had done it all, working in almost every department, mastering every role, and earning more recognition than she'd ever brag about. But even after her diagnosis, she didn't hit the brakes. If anything, she pushed even harder, showing up every day with the same fire and dedication. It was like she was telling cancer; you're not taking this from me. Her perseverance was impressive and downright inspiring.

During her fight with cancer, Stacey finally got the promotion she had long deserved—a chief executive role, a nod to the years of dedication she had poured into the company. But when I saw her at a company conference a few months later, it was clear the battle was taking its toll. Stacey, the woman who had always been so full of life, moved slower now. Her eyes, once bright and full of energy, were dulled with exhaustion. She wore a wig to cover the hair she was losing, and her pale complexion told the story of the brutal treatments she was enduring. And yet, she still showed up. She smiled, she spoke, and she stayed committed, even when it was obvious that every step took everything she had. Just her being there was a testament to her strength.

Then, six months later, Stacey was called into the CEO's office. What happened in that room changed the way I see leadership, loyalty, and the world itself. The conversation started with the usual pleasantries; asking how she was feeling and how her family was holding up. Then, the mood shifted. The CEO thanked her for her years of hard work, acknowledged her sacrifices, and even said the company wouldn't be where it was without her. And then came the gut punch. The words that made my stomach drop. "Unfortunately, Stacey, we have to let you go. It's nothing personal; it's just business."

Twenty years of loyalty, sacrifice, and hard work, all reduced to a cold, impersonal decision. When I heard what had happened, it felt like a punch to the gut. How could they do this to her? How could they just cast her aside after everything she had given? I couldn't stop thinking about it. Stacey's story was heartbreaking and a sad reflection of the world we live in. When did we start valuing profit over people? When did compassion and empathy take a back seat? Have we really become so numb that treating someone as disposable feels normal?

Two weeks after I heard the news, I woke up with a heavy heart. I spent the morning praying for Stacey, hoping she was finding strength in the midst of it all. And then, just eight months later, I got the call that she was gone. Stacey's story unsettled me, challenged me, and made me ask questions I couldn't ignore. Her experience planted a seed in my heart, a seed that would eventually grow into the pages of this book.

The phrase "It's not personal, it's business" kept running through my mind, over and over. How could such a simple sentence justify such cold, heartless decisions? It wasn't just a corporate motto; it had become a mindset that had seeped into every part of society, shaping how we treat each other, even in life's most personal moments. As I wrestled with this, I kept coming back to the words of Isaiah 55:8-9:

*"For my thoughts are not your thoughts, neither are your ways my ways," declares the Lord. "As the heavens are higher than the earth, so are my ways higher than your ways and my thoughts than your thoughts."*

This verse is a clear reminder of just how different God's heart is from the world's way of thinking. The world operates on transactions, but God is all about relationships. But the more I reflected, the more I realized something even more troubling: this transactional way of thinking hasn't just taken over businesses; it has found its way into the church.

Too often, the church operates more like a corporation than a community. Success is measured by numbers, programs, and polished events instead of the depth of relationships or the transformation of lives. When we focus on these types of metrics, we risk losing sight of what the church was meant to be: a family united by love, rooted in God's call to connect deeply and personally with one another.

In a world driven by transactions, the church has a chance, and a responsibility, to be different. The strength of the church doesn't come from systems or strategies; it comes from love. In my journey, I've learned that the strongest sermons aren't the ones preached from pulpits, but the ones lived out in everyday acts of kindness, empathy, and care.

As the world continues to justify its actions with the phrase, "It's not personal, it's just business," the church is called to offer a countercultural response:

"It's not business, it's personal."

This response reflects the very heart of God. His love is never surface level; it's always transformative. When we embrace this calling, we don't just set ourselves apart from the world; we invite others into an experience of love, grace, and connection that can only come from Him. Through authentic relationships, we become a living, breathing expression of God's kingdom—a place where hearts are healed, lives are changed, and the love of Christ is made tangible.

Stacey's story is a reminder of what's at stake. It's a call to reject the superficial, impersonal attitude of the world and embrace the personal, relational heart of the gospel. Because at the end of the day, it's not business, it's personal. And that's exactly how it was always meant to be.

# Introduction

We're living in a whirlwind of constant change, where life seems to demand flexibility at every turn. It's tempting to slip into a rhythm of moving on quickly, whether it's from a job, a friendship, or even a commitment, whenever things get tough or inconvenient. This fast-paced mindset doesn't simply affect the way we shop or consume; it quietly reshapes how we approach our relationships and priorities. Sure, adaptability has its perks, but it can also hold us back from truly investing in what matters most. The things that require long-term commitment, like a meaningful career, deep friendships, or a thriving church community, are becoming harder to find because it's easier to chase what feels convenient or instantly gratifying.

Over time, this way of thinking has slowly slipped into how many of us experience church. Faith starts to feel less like a relationship and more like a transaction. As a result, church becomes something we visit when we need something, instead of a family we belong to. This shift in culture also impacts church leaders, changing how they approach their role and how they define success.

At the same time, members can easily slip into a "checklist" mentality, asking questions like, What's in it for me? Does this fit my schedule? But when we approach church this way, we miss out on its deeper purpose. Church was never meant to be another item on our weekly to-do list. It's designed to be a life-giving community—a place where real love grows, authentic connections are formed, and lasting transformation happens.

James K.A. Smith sums it up so well in *Desiring the Kingdom*:

"When worship is reduced to a commodity, we start to think of ourselves as customers instead of participants in a covenantal relationship with God and His people."

That is a powerful statement. When church becomes a convenience rather than a commitment, we miss the chance to plant deep roots in relationships, accountability, and faith. And without those roots, real, lasting transformation is hard to sustain.

The consumer-first mentality hasn't just shaped the world around us, it's quietly made its way into the church, influencing how we approach ministry. In a culture that craves instant results and polished appearances, it's easy for leaders to feel the pressure to prioritize flashy programs and big events that fill seats, rather than focusing on the kind of spiritual growth that truly changes lives. Don't get me wrong—programs and events have their place. They're valuable tools, but they're not the ultimate goal.

What leaves a lasting impact is authentic connection and intentional discipleship. Yet, when leaders find themselves torn between creating engaging experiences and staying faithful to God's deeper calling, the church's true mission can easily get lost in the shuffle. We are called to save souls and build a Christ-centered, loving community. We can't afford to lose sight of what matters most.

At its core, the church is meant to be so much more than just a building or a calendar full of events. It's a place where people find healing for their hurts, hope for their future, and a sense of belonging that feels like family. Programs and events? They're great tools, no doubt. But their real value shines when they lead us back to God's heart and the relationships, He's calling us to build. A church that truly lives out love in a genuine, connected community becomes a place of real transformation, not because of flashy programs or perfect appearances, but because of the authentic care and connection that flows through every corner. That's what changes lives. That's what makes a church home.

If the church is going to fulfill its calling, we need a bold shift in perspective. We must move from a transactional framework to a relational one, focusing less on numbers and appearances and more on building meaningful, life-giving connections. This isn't a new strategy; it's a return to God's original design for His church.

The church was never meant to feel like a business. It's meant to feel like home—a place where people are embraced with open arms, cared for deeply, and challenged to grow in their faith. It's about reflecting God's love not only in our words, but in the way we live and interact with each other.

Yes, the pull of consumerism is strong, but God's vision for His church is so much greater. He calls us to be a family united by love, living out an authentic faith, and practicing what James describes as "pure and undefiled religion", caring for the vulnerable and putting His love into action (James 1:27). The early church shows us what this looks like. They didn't measure success by the size of their gatherings or the hype around their events. They measured success by their love, service, and support for one another, not by numbers or status. Acts 2:42-47 shows this through their deep fellowship, radical generosity, shared lives, and a unified faith that attracted others to Christ. That's the kind of church we're called to be.

Imagine what would happen if we returned to that kind of community today. What if we saw the church not as a place to consume but as a family to commit to? What if we prioritized people over programs and relationships over routines? It would change everything. People wouldn't just come to church, they'd experience it as a place of transformation, where the love of Christ flows freely and meets them where they are.

This book was born out of a deep desire to see the church return to what it was always meant to be, a place of real relationships. It's a heartfelt call to pastors, leaders, and believers everywhere to let go of the shallow, exchange-based ways of the world and embrace the countercultural values of love, grace, and genuine community. The church is not supposed to be a product we consume or an event we attend. It is a family—a body of believers walking side by side, sharing life, and growing in faith together.

Through these chapters, we'll take a journey into what it means to live as the relational church God envisions. It's about breaking free from the performance-driven, business-like mindset and leaning into love and connection. This isn't a call to do more or pack your schedule, it's about being intentional, about slowing down to truly see and care for the people God has placed in your life.

The challenge is simple, but it's not easy: Will we keep treating church like another thing to check off our to-do list, or will we embrace the deeper, richer calling God has for His people? The choice is ours. We can stay in the comfortable, familiar rhythm of routine-based church life, or we can step boldly into the relational mission God has laid out for us.

When we choose the relational path, something incredible happens. We reflect the heart of Jesus to a world that's starving for hope. We become a family, a community that welcomes the broken, cares for the vulnerable, and shows what love in action really looks like. That's the kind of church that transforms lives. That's the church God is calling us to be.

My prayer is that these words inspire you to embrace that calling. Let's step into the relational church, where we build communities that live out love, not just conceptually, but as a way of life. When the church gets this right, it not only transforms the members, but it also changes the world around them.

# Chapter 1
# The Foundation of a Relational Church

In today's world, especially in Western culture, relationships often feel shallow and transactional. We're so busy chasing success, happiness, and independence that genuine connection and community get pushed aside. It's like we're stuck in a cycle of isolation, where real relationships feel harder to find, and self-centeredness becomes our default setting.

But here's the truth: the way we connect with others is central to who we are and how we thrive. Real connections lift our spirits, strengthen our mental health, support our physical well-being, and even extend our lives. Research shows that meaningful relationships can lower anxiety, boost immunity, and increase longevity. That's the power of true-hearted connections.

On the flip side, when those connections are missing or broken, the impact can be devastating. *A 2010 meta-analysis published in PLOS Medicine by psychologist Dr. Julianne Holt-Lunstad* found that social isolation and weak relationships increase the risk of premature death as much as smoking 15 cigarettes a day. Further reinforcing this, Holt-Lunstad presented additional findings at the 2017 American Psychological Association Convention, emphasizing the significant health risks of loneliness and disconnection. Let that sink in.

It doesn't stop there—broken relationships ripple out, affecting trust, unity, and our sense of shared purpose. Whether it's how we raise our kids or how we tackle challenges as a community, relationships are the foundation of it all. That's how deeply they matter.

Even studies from places like Harvard confirm this truth, people feel lonelier than ever, despite being constantly connected online. What was meant to bring us closer is often what leaves us more isolated. Instead of fostering real, deep connections, they push us to present polished, curated versions of ourselves. And what happens? We feel more distant, unseen, and disconnected than ever. In a world that worships productivity, it's easy to lose sight of what truly matters, building deep, lasting relationships with the people around us.

It's difficult to accept, but many of our relationships are driven by convenience, what someone can do for us or how they fit into our plans, rather than rooted in love, grace, and genuine commitment. The communities that once gave us a sense of belonging are fading, leaving people scattered. This is an epidemic and a sobering reminder that the connection we desire can't be found in a perfectly filtered photo or a quick comment online. It's found in the kind of relationships that truly go deep.

Relationships can be tough; there's no denying that. Sometimes, they feel downright exhausting. But why? For many of us, it comes down to fear. Fear of being vulnerable. Fear of letting someone see the unpolished, imperfect parts of us we would rather keep hidden. Maybe it's because we've been hurt before, and trusting again feels like too big a risk. Or maybe it's the culture around us, one that glorifies independence and self-reliance, making it seem like needing others is a sign of weakness.

Those fears and wounds, as real as they are, only stand in the way of something far more beautiful. When we hold back from deeper connections, we're not protecting ourselves, we're missing out. True connection doesn't require us to have it all together. It happens when we're willing to step into the messy, vulnerable, and sometimes uncomfortable process of being fully seen and fully known. And that's where real growth and healing begin.

C.S. Lewis captured this so powerfully when he wrote, "Friendship… is born at the moment when one person says to another, 'What! You too? I thought I was the only one.'" (*The Four Loves*, 1960). Isn't that what we're all craving? Those moments where someone truly gets us, where we realize we're not alone in what we're feeling or facing. That's the beauty of real relationships; they remind us that we were never meant to do life on our own.

When genuine love and unity are missing from our lives, the effects can be felt everywhere. Relationships become strained, leaving people feeling misunderstood and undervalued. When self-interest takes the lead, and people begin relating to one another out of convenience or personal gain, trust begins to fade, and meaningful connections become harder to find. In this kind of environment, judgment takes the place of compassion, bitterness thrives where forgiveness is absent, and competition overshadows true community.

The damage goes beyond our personal lives; it impacts the way we function as a society. Loneliness grows, anxiety deepens, and divisions widen. Instead of building connections, people start to operate from a place of self-preservation, focusing on protecting themselves rather than making sacrifices for others. This way of seeing things builds walls where there should be bridges, leaving us more disconnected from one another than ever before.

## When the Church Mirrors the World

Unfortunately, the church isn't immune to the fallout when Godly affection and unity are set aside. When a community is built on duty, performance, or status instead of authentic relationships, it begins to reflect the world's transactional mindset, losing sight of what Jesus taught us about true connection. For example, when volunteers are valued more for their efficiency than their well-being, service becomes a transaction rather than an act of love. Instead of fostering connection, the church risks becoming a place where people are used for their gifts but neglected in their struggles.

Real community is messy, it just is. It's not this picture-perfect group where everyone always gets along or agrees on everything. If you've spent any time in a close community, you know that personalities clash. Maybe someone says something hurtful without even realizing it, or you find yourself frustrated because you see things so differently. And then there are the moments when forgiveness feels impossible, when the hurt cuts deep, and you're tempted to just walk away.

> *when volunteers are valued more for their efficiency than their well-being, service becomes a transaction rather than an act of love*

Yet it is in those messy moments where the real beauty of community can shine. It is in those challenges that we have the chance to love the way Jesus taught us to choose grace, patience, and understanding when it would be so much easier to give up. Think of Peter asking Jesus how many times he should forgive someone. Jesus responds, not seven times, but seventy-seven times seven (Matthew 18:21-22). He was teaching us that forgiveness isn't a one-time act; it's a commitment to keep showing up, even when it's tough.

That's what makes a Kingdom family. It's not about everything being perfect; it's about staying faithful to each other in the imperfections. It's about saying, "I'm here, and I'm not going anywhere," even when things get messy. That kind of commitment builds trust, and trust is the foundation for relationships that last. Commitment matters, especially when it's hard.

Christine Pohl, in *Living into Community*, gives us a powerful yet practical reminder about what it takes to build real, lasting connections. She highlights simple but essential practices like gratitude and truth-telling. They might not sound flashy, but they're foundational.

Gratitude has a way of shifting our perspective. Instead of focusing on the ways people might annoy or disappoint us, it helps us see them as gifts. It opens our eyes to the small, everyday moments where others show up for us, even in the middle of life's chaos.

But gratitude alone isn't enough, true connection also requires honesty. Without truth-telling and truth-living, relationships can't thrive. Pretending, avoiding hard conversations, or hiding behind masks only creates distance. Truth-telling, on the other hand, builds trust. It allows us to show up as our authentic selves, knowing we'll still be loved and accepted for who we really are.

Pohl challenges us to move beyond simply *thinking* about these things and start *living* them daily. Gratitude and truth-telling ground us in love and keep us connected. They remind us that community isn't about finding perfect people. Community is about choosing faithfulness. It's about a kind of commitment towards one another that is anchored in God's love, making relationships truly meaningful.

## More Than Just a Building

The church is meant to be a home, a place where authentic relationships give people a deep sense of belonging and purpose. It's where we are truly seen, valued, and supported. The church was designed to reflect God's relational nature, bringing people together in unity and purpose. When we live this out, we're not merely talking about the gospel, we're living it. This is love in action.

At its core, our faith isn't about checking items off a list or looking the part. It's about letting God's love transform every part of who we are. It's about building relationships. When we truly love God, that love overflows and begins to shape how we treat others. Real connection and unity happen when love is at the center of everything we do.

This is the very foundation of our relationship with God and with others. It's through love that we discover who God is, who we are, and how we're called to live in community. Whether personal or spiritual, everything in life revolves around relationships—and at the center of it all is our relationship with God.

Our relationship with God shapes how we connect with others and influences the way we engage with the world. It is this connection with Him that lays the foundation for a relational church—one that embodies His love through intentionality and unity.

*But what does it mean to love God with our whole being, and how does that love shape our relationships with others?*

Jesus already gave us the answer in Mark 12, love God fully and love your neighbor as yourself. These two commandments are the foundation of everything, shaping how we live and lead in relationship.

These words are more than guidelines; they're an invitation to live a life defined by relational unity. An invitation to live a life that embodies the love of God not only in our worship but also in how we treat those around us. This is where the journey of a relational church begins: with a heart committed to loving God fully, allowing His love to overflow into every aspect of our lives, especially our relationships. N.T. Wright puts it this way: Christian love calls us to "live as a community of love, showing the world that this is the life God wants for us" (*Simply Christian*, 2006). Ultimately, the goal is to build a church rooted in love, driven by a true desire for connection, unity, and grace.

## The Foundation of Our Faith: Loving God and Others

The command to love God with all our heart, soul, mind, and strength, and to love our neighbors as ourselves, is the heartbeat of Christianity, the thread that weaves together our relationship with God and our connection to others. As Timothy Keller so beautifully says, "The Christian understanding of love is based on the principle that true love is sacrificial, unconditional, and focused on the other" (*The Meaning of Marriage*, 2011).

When we truly love God, it completely changes how we see people. Relationships are no longer optional or based on convenience, they're part of a divine calling, central to the purpose God has for us. Every person becomes a reflection of His image, deserving of value, grace, and care. Loving God with everything we are, compels us to extend that same grace, patience, and kindness to those around us. It invites us to live in a way where relationships are important and sacred.

Vertical intimacy with God fuels horizontal relationships with others. And these connections become the spaces where God's love shows up in tangible ways. This kind of love transforms how we interact with our families, how we engage with our communities, and how we connect with our church.

We're no longer isolated individuals trying to navigate life alone. Instead, we become part of something much greater, a community knit together by God's love and driven by a shared purpose. This unity is the heartbeat of a relational church, a church that rejects the pull of individualism and instead builds a community where the well-being of others is just as important as our own.

> *Vertical intimacy with God fuels horizontal relationships with others.*

When Jesus spoke about the two greatest commandments, He wasn't just giving us rules to follow; He was painting a vision of what the kingdom of God looks like. It's a kingdom where love breaks down walls, crosses cultural divides, and brings people together from every walk of life. In a world obsessed with independence and self-reliance, Jesus shows us that true fulfillment isn't found in isolation but in connection—with God and with one another. His words challenge us to live a life where love takes the lead, transforming not only our lives but the world around us.

## Love as the Foundation of Unity

One of the most beautiful truths of our faith is that love is the glue holding us together, creating true unity. But this unity can't be shallow or surface-level. Unity is formed through love, beyond shared beliefs or lifestyles. It goes much deeper, reflecting the very heart of God. In John 17, Jesus prays, *"I pray that they may be one as we are one"* (John 17:22). Love is heaven's native language. It's what shapes true unity and draws us deeper into God's heart. Think about that, Jesus is asking for His followers to embody a unity that mirrors God's divine harmony. That's not casual agreement; it's a unity built on love, mutual respect, and a shared purpose.

This kind of unity is rooted in the kind of love that honors and values each person's unique gifts and contributions. It's a love that cares about the well-being of the whole body of Christ, not just individual members. When love becomes our foundation, unity naturally follows. It's what happens when a church prioritizes relationships over routines and connections over programs.

As Francis Chan writes in *Crazy Love* (2008), "We are most alive when we are loving and actively giving ourselves because we were made to do these things." In this kind of community, everyone matters, and every relationship plays a vital role. This unity not only draws us closer to one another but also aligns us with God's heart, reflecting the richness and diversity of His family.

In a relational church, unity is not about conformity, it's about celebrating our differences while staying anchored in our shared love for God and each other. This love-centered unity transforms the church into more than a gathering place; it becomes a home, a family where everyone feels seen, valued, and deeply connected. Unity here is about letting go of self-centeredness. It's a place where no one is just an attendee or participant, they're an essential part of something greater, bound together by the love of Christ.

## Practical Expressions of Relational Unity

Relational unity doesn't happen by accident; it takes more than good intentions. It requires action: intentional, consistent steps to build relationships that reflect God's love. This is what sets a relational church apart from a group of people gathering for events or programs. It's through these deliberate acts of love and care that God's presence becomes real and tangible in our community.

Loving others well means truly showing up in their lives, not only physically, but emotionally and spiritually. It's about listening without rushing to conclusions, offering support without expecting anything in return, and standing with people in both their joy and their pain. It means choosing grace over judgment when conflicts arise and pursuing reconciliation with humility, even when it's difficult. Love that looks like Jesus' love requires effort and sacrifice.

In practice, this might look like reaching out to someone who's struggling, inviting someone over for a meal who feels lonely, or simply taking time to connect deeply with someone in the congregation. It's about noticing people, really seeing them, and letting them know they matter. These small, intentional acts of love create a ripple effect, shaping an environment where people feel valued and supported.

It's in these moments, shared meals, heartfelt conversations, and simple acts of kindness, that a church becomes more than a building or a Sunday service. It becomes a family, a place where everyone knows they belong.

## Love Is the Church's Greatest Witness

When Jesus said, *"By this everyone will know that you are my disciples, if you love one another"* (John 13:35), He wasn't merely offering a nice idea to strive for. He was giving us our identity. Love is meant to set us apart. It's the unmistakable mark of who we are as His people.

Even in Jesus' time, people were drawn to status, appearances, and external displays of devotion. Yet His words cut through all of that, emphasizing that true discipleship isn't defined by impressive buildings, flawless programs, or eloquent sermons, it's defined by love. That was true then, and it's just as true today. Love is the foundation that speaks louder than words, revealing the heart of the gospel.

There's something undeniably powerful about a community where love isn't just preached, but it's practiced in real, life-changing ways. When people choose to show up for one another with compassion and intentionality, lives are changed. Love that steps in, stands beside, and sacrifices restores dignity, revives hope, and reflects the heart of God in the most tangible ways. This kind of love not only impacts the one receiving it but it also shows the world what's possible when the church truly becomes the hands and feet of Jesus.

When love becomes the church's identity, it breaks down stereotypes and challenges the misconceptions so many people have about Christians. Some people think the church is all about judgment or rigid rules, while others see it as irrelevant or out of touch. But love tears down those walls. It doesn't have to be flashy or complicated to be powerful. When people experience a love that's patient, kind, and unconditional, it disarms their doubts and invites them to see the church—and God—in a completely new way.

When the church fully embraces this kind of love, it becomes a refuge and a beacon of hope. This love is magnetic; it draws people in, not because of grand events or polished presentations, but because of the authenticity of a community that genuinely cares. It's through this kind of love; visible, active, and unconditional, that the church fulfills its mission. It shows the world a God who not only loves but transforms lives, inviting everyone to experience His grace, compassion, and power.

## A Vision for the Relational Church

In a world full of noise and nonstop interaction, many of us still feel unknown. What we truly long for are the kinds of relationships that touch the soul, where presence matters more than performance. Yet we often find ourselves engaging in these hollow connections that fail to meet the longing God placed in us for real, authentic relationships.

Jesus offered us a radically different way. His relationships weren't shallow; they were deeply personal and intentional. He didn't simply speak to crowds; He sat with individuals, looked into their eyes, called them by name, and invited them into something deeper. Think about His encounter with Zacchaeus, the tax collector everyone despised. Jesus didn't just notice Zacchaeus from a distance, nor did He preach to him. Instead, He said, *"Come down. I must stay at your house today"* (Luke 19:5). That single act of love and intentionality changed Zacchaeus' life forever.

This is the kind of connection Jesus modeled. It's a connection that says, "You matter, not because of what you do, but because of who you are." A relational church reflects this heart. It's a place where people feel genuinely seen and not judged by their appearance. It's a community built on trust, empathy, and grace, a place that feels like family.

The relational church is one where love lies at the very center of everything it does. Love isn't a word to be tossed around in passing, it's the foundation and driving force behind every action, decision, and interaction. In this kind of church, relationships matter more than rituals. It's not merely a gathering place; it's a spiritual home where people are unconditionally loved. This vision challenges us to move beyond the surface-level connections of today's world and embrace the kind of deep relationships Jesus modeled. It's a unity that changes how we relate to one another and reflects God's love.

Now, contrast that with a church that prioritizes performance. When the focus shifts to appearances, flawless programs, polished worship sets, and getting everything "right", something crucial is lost. People begin to feel like they have to earn their place instead of being welcomed for who they are.

However, in a relational church, love takes center stage, and everything changes. The message becomes, "Come as you are. You're welcome here, not because of what you bring, but because you belong." In that kind of community, people experience the fullness of God's love, a love that transforms lives in ways nothing else can.

A relational church radiates love so powerfully and authentically that it draws people closer to God through every interaction. It allows God's love to flow through us in ways that bring healing, unity, and transformation to the world around us.

That's the kind of love that changes everything.

## Embracing the Call to Love

As we wrap up this first chapter, let's take a moment to reflect on what it truly means to live out a relational faith. Hebrews 13 offers us a powerful roadmap—a call to action that goes beyond words and invites us to embody God's love. *"Keep on loving one another as brothers and sisters. Do not forget to show hospitality to strangers… And do not forget to do good and to share with others, for with such sacrifices God is pleased"* (Hebrews 13:1-2, 16). These aren't gentle suggestions; they're bold declarations of what a life shaped by love looks like in action.

Now, imagine a community where these words were the very fabric of daily life. Picture a church where love fuels every conversation, every gathering, and every decision. Imagine a space where people walk in and immediately feel like they belong, where no one slips through the cracks, and where every act of kindness speaks volumes, louder than any sermon could. That's the heartbeat of a relational church, a place where God's love is more than a topic of discussion. It's seen, felt, and experienced in tangible, life-changing ways.

But a love like this requires more than words. It calls us to live differently. It asks us to step beyond convenience, beyond comfort, and embrace the hard, holy work of relationship. It's not about getting it all right; it's about showing up with persistence.

The call to love is the call to live beyond ourselves. Are we willing to sacrifice our time, preferences, and even our pride to love others the way Jesus asks us to? Are we ready to trade shallow connections for deep, transformative relationships? These are the questions that will shape not only our churches but our lives.

This is where the journey begins. As we move into the next chapters, we'll unpack what it looks like to bring these truths to life. We'll explore how to prioritize love over performance, how to build relationships that last, and how to foster a church culture that truly reflects God's heart.

The path ahead won't always be easy, but it will be worth it; because love, real love, has the power to change everything. So, as you turn the page, ask yourself: *What would it look like for me, for my church, for my family, for my community to make love the foundation of everything we do?*

The answers to that question could change how you see the church, how you see others, and even how you see yourself. And that's where the real adventure begins.

# Chapter 2
# Beyond Performance and Rituals

## The Weight of Spiritual Expectations

Have you ever felt like your faith was being measured by how much you do rather than how well you know God? It's a common struggle, one that often goes unnoticed because it's woven so deeply into church culture. Without realizing it, many believers slip into a belief system where spiritual performance becomes the standard of faithfulness. The more visible you are, the more active you are, the more spiritual you must be, at least, that's the unspoken expectation.

This is where the Pygmalion Effect comes into play—both in psychology and in faith. The Pygmalion effect is a concept suggesting that people tend to rise (or fall) to the level of expectations placed on them. If a leader believes in someone's potential, that belief often fuels confidence and growth. But when expectations become less about encouragement and more about proving worth, they can create a culture of striving, one where people feel pressured to constantly *do more* to be considered faithful.

Over time, these expectations become deeply ingrained, shaping not only how people serve but also how they see their spiritual worth. Church cultures that emphasize high expectations can unintentionally create a performance-based faith, where people feel valuable only when they're actively producing. It's a silent pressure, one that leads many to believe that slowing down means falling behind. Or, that if they aren't constantly meeting the bar, they're somehow failing spiritually.

While this may be well-intended, it can lead to a subtle but dangerous attitude shift. One where faith becomes more about meeting expectations than about knowing God intimately. It's easy to equate busyness with devotion, productivity with spirituality, and service with closeness to God. Before long, people find themselves exhausted, overcommitted, and still wondering if they're doing *enough*.

But here's the real danger: this posture makes our relationship with God feel mechanical. If we're not careful, we start believing that His love, approval, and blessings are things we must *earn* rather than *receive*. And when faith becomes a performance rather than a relationship, we drift from the very intimacy with God for which we were created. But Faith isn't about appearances; it's about authentic connection with God.

So how do we recognize when spiritual performance is replacing real connection? And, more importantly, how do we move beyond it? That's where the longing for authentic intimacy with God comes in—something we all crave, yet so often struggle to find.

# The Tension Between Church Involvement and Spiritual Growth

In many church cultures, faithfulness is often measured by visibility. The ones who serve the most, lead the most, and take on the most responsibility are often seen as the most spiritually mature. It's an unspoken expectation. If you're truly committed to God, you'll stay busy in His house. And because of the way expectations shape us, people naturally internalize this idea, believing that the more active they are, the stronger their faith must be. But over time, this mentality creates a dangerous pattern: people begin confusing spiritual activity with spiritual growth.

This subtle shift is hard to notice at first. It feels good to be involved, to be needed, to be part of something bigger than yourself. But when busyness becomes the standard of faithfulness, it's easy to assume that doing more automatically means becoming more. Many people spend years engaged in church work yet struggle with the nagging feeling that something is missing.

We are wired with a deep desire for meaning, an internal drive to know that what we're doing actually matters. But what happens when the very thing we expect to fulfill us leaves us feeling drained instead? What happens when being present in every service, attending every leadership meeting, and taking on every opportunity still doesn't satisfy the deeper questions stirring inside us?

This is the tension so many believers wrestle with: if I'm doing everything right, why does it still feel like something is off? It's a question many don't know how to ask. So instead, they pour themselves deeper into the work, hoping that, eventually, the feeling will go away.

This is where we need to take a step back and ask ourselves: Has church culture unintentionally placed more value on outward involvement than on inward transformation? Have we created an environment where people feel pressured to be seen rather than challenged to grow? If so, we may need to rethink what true spiritual growth really looks like. It can't just be about how much we do, it has to be about something much deeper.

## Redefining Spiritual Depth in a Culture of Recognition

Some of the most dedicated people in church are also the ones struggling the most. Not because they lack faith or commitment, but because they've unknowingly tied their spiritual identity to what they do rather than who they are in Christ. When serving becomes the primary measure of faithfulness, it's easy to believe that as long as we're busy, we're growing. But over time, this mindset leads to exhaustion, not transformation.

Not long ago, I was talking with a young woman who shared something that caught my attention. She said, "I feel closest to God when I serve because I was taught that serving brings me nearer to Him." When I asked why she believed that, she paused, thought for a moment, and then admitted, "I'm not really sure, that's just the way I was taught."

Her words stuck with me because I understood exactly what she meant. For years, I had lived the same way, believing that the more I did for God, the closer I must be to Him. I equated my busyness with spiritual depth, assuming that if I was constantly leading, serving, and showing up, I was growing. But looking back, I see how easy it is to mistake ministry involvement for personal transformation.

When our identity becomes wrapped up in what we do for God, we risk losing sight of what matters most—who we are in Him. Spiritual growth isn't about how many roles we take on; it's about what's happening in our hearts. And if we're not careful, we can spend years busy in the house of God but distant from the presence of God. When we prioritize presence over performance, we encounter the fullness of who HE is.

This pattern has existed for generations. Even in biblical times, people were shaped by the expectations placed upon them. Like today, they had to navigate the tension between outward religious practice and true spiritual depth. The Pygmalion Effect may be a modern term, but the reality of its influence can be traced throughout scripture.

This struggle isn't new. Even in the Old Testament, people had to learn the difference between knowing about God and knowing God personally. One of the clearest examples of this is found in Samuel's life.

## Lessons from the Life of Samuel

When I reflect on what it truly means to move beyond performance and rituals, the story of young Samuel in 1 Samuel chapter 3 stands out. Samuel's journey didn't begin when he entered the temple, it started with a desperate, heartfelt prayer from his mother, Hannah. She cried out to God, pleading for a child, and in her desperation, she made a bold vow: if God blessed her with a son, she would dedicate him entirely to His service.

When that moment came, Hannah kept her promise. She brought Samuel to the temple and entrusted him to Eli, the priest, fulfilling her vow with unwavering faith. Imagine the depth of her surrender; offering back to God the very child she had longed for and prayed over. It was an act of obedience and a testament to a lifelong trust in God's plan.

Samuel's upbringing was anything but easy. He grew up in a temple environment marred by spiritual compromise. Eli's sons, Hophni and Phinehas, who also served in the temple, were far from godly. They abused their positions, dishonored God's offerings, and exploited their roles for personal gain. Samuel, still just a boy, saw their hypocrisy up close. Yet, despite being surrounded by corruption, Samuel stood out. He remained faithful, humble, and wholeheartedly devoted to God.

Scripture paints a beautiful picture of this: "The boy Samuel continued to grow in stature and favor with the Lord and with people" (1 Samuel 2:26). Even in the middle of a broken system, Samuel's life reminds us that what God truly values is not how perfectly we follow rituals, but the sincerity and posture of our hearts.

## The Value of Serving in God's House

Samuel's story illustrates how serving God is not only an act of obedience but a vital part of our spiritual journey. From a young age, Samuel ministered to the Lord under Eli's guidance, immersing himself in the written Word and faithfully serving in the temple. His life shows how serving shapes our character and refines our hearts.

Serving in God's house isn't about fulfilling a role, it's about what happens inside of us as we do. Beyond the tasks themselves, serving brings spiritual benefits that shape us in profound ways:

- **Builds Character:** Serving instills responsibility, discipline, and commitment, shaping us into people who honor God in every aspect of life.

- **Reveals the Heart:** Service has a way of exposing our true intentions and motivations, giving us the chance to grow in self-awareness and integrity.
- **Develops Humility:** In God's kingdom, no task is too small. Whether it's sweeping the floors or leading a ministry, every role is significant and valuable.
- **Fosters Connection:** Serving deepens our understanding of the church's heart and the needs of the people around us, building genuine community.
- **Provides Growth Opportunities:** Stepping into service often pushes us beyond our comfort zones, helping us grow spiritually and discover new gifts.
- **Earns Favor with God and People:** Genuine service reflects love and dedication, leaving a lasting impression on others and bringing joy to God's heart.
- **Demonstrates Commitment and Maturity:** Serving shows a heart fully devoted to God, ready to embrace greater responsibilities and deeper spiritual growth.

As essential as serving is for spiritual development, it can never replace intimacy with God. No amount of serving could ever produce the intimacy required to identify God's voice. But what serving does is it positions us to respond to His call when it comes.

This truth is so evident in Samuel's story. While Samuel served faithfully in the temple, Eli and his sons were dishonoring God and tarnishing their roles as priests. Yet even in the middle of that broken and corrupt environment, Samuel remained faithful in his serving. It was in the midst of his service that God called him by name.

What's interesting about this story is that Samuel heard the voice but didn't recognize who's voice he was hearing. It took three

> No amount of serving could ever produce the intimacy required to identify God's voice.

calls, and Eli's guidance before Samuel finally understood that it was God speaking to him.

The first time God called Samuel, he immediately ran to Eli, thinking it was Eli's voice he had heard. But Eli shook his head and sent him back to bed, saying, "It wasn't me." A second time, Samuel heard the voice, and again, he ran to Eli, only to hear the same response. On the third call, Samuel once more ran to Eli, but this time, something clicked. Eli realized what was happening and instructed Samuel, "If the voice calls again, say, 'Speak, Lord, for Your servant is listening.'"

Samuel's faithful service had prepared him for this pivotal moment. Yet, it also revealed several important truths: knowing *about* God and working in His house is not the same as truly *knowing* Him, and God is not impressed by rituals but moved by genuine surrender. It was in this encounter with God's voice that Samuel's personal, intimate relationship with the Lord began. This moment serves as a powerful reminder that while serving is vital, it's meant to deepen our connection with God, not replace it. Simply being active in ministry isn't enough; we must also cultivate the ability to recognize His voice.

This theme runs throughout Scripture. God consistently calls His people to move beyond surface-level rituals and into deeper relationships. In Isaiah 58, He rebukes Israel for their hollow practices, urging them to focus instead on justice, mercy, and love. Like Samuel, the people of Israel were reminded that God doesn't seek mere activity, He desires authentic connection.

Samuel lived in the temple, sleeping near the Ark of the Covenant, the very symbol of God's presence, yet he didn't recognize God's voice when it called. This story also highlights a sobering truth: it's entirely possible to be surrounded by sacred things and still miss the intimacy God desires. Despite Samuel's faithfulness and dedication, he hadn't yet developed the relationship necessary to discern the Lord's call. This distinction is humbling and eye-opening; serving, no matter how diligent or committed, isn't a substitute for intimacy with God.

## When Serving Becomes a Substitute

This leads to one of the most subtle yet dangerous traps in the "Christian Walk": mistaking busyness in ministry for closeness with God. It's a pitfall we rarely talk about, but it's all too common. A.W. Tozer captured it perfectly in *The Pursuit of God* when he wrote, "The world is perishing for lack of the knowledge of God, and the Church is famishing for want of His Presence" (1948).

This is a critique and a wake-up call. We can fill our schedules with ministry work and yet still find ourselves spiritually starved if we neglect the deeper intimacy God longs for.

I know this trap well. Growing up, I was involved in nearly every aspect of church life—leading worship, teaching classes, preaching sermons, and even cleaning floors. I believed that my level of activity directly reflected my spiritual closeness to God. The busier I was, the more faithful I felt. But looking back, I see how easily I equated *doing* for God with *being* close to Him. My focus shifted from connection to performance, and I wore my busyness as a badge of honor.

This is one of the enemy's most effective strategies. If he can't stop us from serving, he'll redirect our focus so that our service becomes an end in itself. We get caught up in planning events, managing programs, and perfecting presentations, all while losing sight of what truly matters.

The lights, the production, the tasks, they're not bad, but if they pull us away from intimacy with God, they've missed their purpose. The enemy knows that sometimes the best way to keep us from pursuing God is to keep us busy with "good" things that leave us spiritually empty.

Samuel's story underscores this truth. He was diligent, faithful, and fully immersed in temple life, yet he didn't initially recognize God's voice. 1 Samuel 3:7 captures this with a simple yet profound statement: "Now Samuel did not yet <u>know</u> the Lord, nor had the word of the Lord been revealed to him." That phrase, "did not yet know the Lord," is key. Samuel's service, while commendable, wasn't enough to cultivate the intimacy he needed to truly know God.

The word "know" in this passage carries deep significance. It's the same word Mary uses in Luke 1:34 when she asks the angel, *"How can this be, since I <u>know</u> no man?"* In this context, "know" refers to an intimate, personal relationship, not a surface-level connection. Similarly, in Matthew 7:22-23, Jesus delivers a sobering message: *"Many will say to me on that day, 'Lord, Lord, did we not prophesy in Your name, and in Your name drive out demons and perform many miracles?' Then I will tell them plainly, 'I never <u>knew</u> you. Away from me, you evildoers!'"*

How could the God who created us say, "I never knew you?". Jesus isn't talking about intellectual knowledge, He's talking about a deep, transformative relationship. Just as Samuel had to move beyond his duties in the temple to truly know the Lord, we, too, must move beyond activity to foster genuine intimacy with God.

This kind of intimacy requires more than service. It demands stillness, vulnerability, and a willingness to not only hear God's voice but also discern that it is Him who is speaking. Truly knowing God deeply shapes intimacy more than serving ever could.

## Cultivating Real Intimacy with God

If the only time you crack open your Bible is when the preacher says, "Let's turn to this passage," you're missing the richness of knowing Him personally. Intimacy with God isn't formed in occasional moments or shared public settings, it grows through a consistent, private connection.

If the only time you pray is during a church service, how can a real closeness with Him take root? A genuine relationship with God means daily conversation, pouring out your heart, and creating space to hear His voice. If the only time you lift your hands in worship is during a corporate set, you're holding back from fully encountering Him.

Our lives reflect what we consistently make time for. We can't claim to love God if He never makes it onto our schedule. Intimacy is nurtured through time spent with Him, through a deep, ongoing relationship that welcomes God into every part of our lives.

The closer we draw to God, the more He fills us, enlarging our capacity to carry His purpose and walk in His authority. But when intimacy is absent, our spiritual capacity shrinks, and so does our ability to move in the authority He's given us. Too often, we miss out on the fullness of God's plans because we haven't taken the time to truly know Him.

When we lack a personal connection with God, we often settle for outward substitutes; programs, strategies, and polished services that simulate growth but don't foster deep transformation. These things might capture attention for a while, but they can't create the kind of relationship that leads to lasting spiritual growth. This is a reality

> *We can't claim to love God if He never makes it onto our schedule.*

in many churches today. People have become reliant on external motivators; dynamic worship sets, eloquent sermons, and impressive programs—to feel connected to God.

While these all have their place, they can never replace the inward transformation that only comes from a real relationship with Him. It's easier to orchestrate a flawless service than to invite God into the raw, unpolished places in our hearts. Yet true change happens in those vulnerable, surrendered moments.

## The Power of Private Worship

Real intimacy with God isn't about what happens on Sunday mornings or how flawless we appear in front of others. It's not measured by public acts of service, eloquent prayers, or the perception of a perfect faith. True intimacy is cultivated in the quiet, hidden moments, the times when no one else is watching.

Jesus speaks directly to this in Matthew 6:1: *"Be careful not to practice your righteousness in front of others to be seen by them. If you do, you will have no reward from your Father in heaven."* This verse reminds us that our relationship with God isn't meant to be a performance; it's meant to be deeply personal and real. When we get caught up in playing the part rather than connecting with Him authentically, we miss out on the profound joy and reward of a genuine relationship with our Creator.

When our focus shifts from *who* we are doing it for to *what* we are doing, God can easily become secondary in our lives. In this misplaced focus, we often lean on external triggers to feel close to Him. Whether it's the emotional high of a worship service, a powerful song, or an impactful event, we sometimes treat these moments as replacements for daily, personal intimacy with God.

John Piper puts it beautifully in *Desiring God*: *"God is most glorified in us when we are most satisfied in Him"* (1986). The problem is, we often act like God isn't enough on His own. We scramble to make the gospel feel more entertaining or engaging, as though His presence alone is not sufficient. Yet if we truly grasped the depth of His love and the fullness of His presence, we would realize that nothing else could ever compare. His presence alone is more than enough.

God calls us to cultivate a deeper relationship through daily encounters with His Word and His Spirit. When He becomes the center of our lives, the need for external motivators fades, and we begin to experience the peace and joy of knowing that He is more than sufficient. The gospel doesn't need flashy packaging or modern upgrades to remain relevant. Its power is in its simplicity: God's presence, transforming our hearts and lives. When we root ourselves in Him, we discover the intimacy, satisfaction, and purpose that no program, event, or performance could ever replicate.

We live in a culture that celebrates the curated, polished version of ourselves. We hide behind "spiritual" busyness, filling our schedules with activities and actions that mask a lack of true relationship with God. If we're not careful, we can fall into the trap of believing that ministry involvement or church attendance automatically translates to spiritual closeness. Outward productivity doesn't necessarily mean we're nurturing an inward, genuine relationship with Him.

To truly experience intimacy with God, we have to let go of the performance and move beyond the rituals. God isn't looking for a curated, filtered version of us—He wants our raw, unpolished, and authentic selves. This level of connection requires surrender.

It means coming to Him with open hearts, ready to release our agendas, our plans, and our need to maintain control. It means holding nothing back and giving Him access to every part of our lives, the good, the messy, and the broken. It's in this kind of vulnerable surrender that true intimacy is found. God doesn't ask for perfection; He asks for our hearts. Relational depth begins not in doing more, but in giving Him everything.

## God's Pursuit

From the very beginning, God designed us to live in deep, intimate connection with Him. This relationship is woven into the very essence of who we are and why we exist. Being part of the church isn't primarily about witnessing miracles, though they beautifully display God's power.

It's not just about celebrating the accomplishments of people who feel unqualified, though we're inspired by the way God equips those who feel least prepared, just as He did time and again throughout Scripture. While these things encourage and uplift us, at its core, our faith is about something far greater: a personal, life-giving relationship with God, our Creator, our Father, and the One who loves us beyond measure.

God's love for us is both overwhelming and unwavering. It's a love so profound that He sent His only Son to die for us, restoring the relationship that sin had broken. This love isn't passive or conditional. It's active, steadfast, and overflowing with grace. Even when we fall short, turn away, or deny Him in our weakness, He remains faithful, always inviting us back with open arms. His greatest desire is that we know Him, not as a distant or detached deity, but as a loving Father who wants to walk with us through every moment of our lives.

Just as God called Samuel into a deeper purpose, He calls each of us into a relationship that transcends rituals and routines. This isn't about simply knowing facts about God; it's about truly knowing Him. It's about walking in His love and allowing it to reshape every part of who we are.

This kind of relationship is for our benefit; but it's also meant to ripple outward and touch the lives of others. When we live closely connected to God, His love, joy, and peace naturally flow through us, drawing others to Him. Our connection with God becomes a vibrant, living testimony that reveals His heart through the way we love, serve, and share our lives with those around us.

As we deepen our understanding of God's love, we're compelled to share it. This is the heartbeat of the Great Commission: *"Go and make disciples of all nations"* (Matthew 28:19). This isn't just a call to preach or teach. It's a call to embody His love in practical, everyday ways. When we encounter the goodness of God, it transforms us, and that transformation spills over into every relationship and interaction.

Our lives become living, breathing demonstrations of His grace, kindness, and mercy. As followers of Christ, we're not only called to tell people about His love; we're called to show it, in how we treat others, how we serve, and how we carry His presence into every space we enter.

When we do this, we create opportunities for others to step into His light and experience the same life-changing love we've found. Our journey with God becomes far more than a personal story. It becomes an open invitation for others to encounter Him. Through us, they see the hope, peace, and fullness of life that only He can offer. In living this way, we reflect His heart and fulfill His purpose, making His love known to the world around us.

# Chapter 3
# Moving Beyond Self-Centeredness

## When Doing Replaces Being

When faith becomes a checklist and serving turns into striving, it's only a matter of time before our hearts begin to shift. What starts as a desire to honor God can slowly morph into a subtle, inward focus, a need to prove ourselves, to be seen, to feel significant.

We may not even realize it, but performance-based faith can create a quiet undercurrent of self-centeredness. Instead of being fueled by intimacy with God, we're driven by affirmation and recognition. And over time, we start measuring our worth by what we do, how much we contribute, and how others perceive us. It's a dangerous drift, not toward rebellion, but toward self.

When the doing outweighs the being, our hearts begin to revolve around our image, our agenda, and our reputation. The result?

We start living from a place of self-protection instead of self-sacrifice. If we're not careful, spiritual performance can lead us to a faith that looks good on the outside but is disconnected from the heart of God. That's why moving beyond performance must also lead us to confront the self-centeredness it quietly breeds.

What begins as devotion can turn into self-focus when we aren't careful. We can get so wrapped up in doing things *for* God that we forget to walk *with* God—and in the process, we begin to center our faith around ourselves. Our prayers, our goals, our service, all of it subtly shifts toward self-preservation and self-importance. It's not always pride; sometimes, it's pain or fear that leads us there.

Regardless of the reason, when our faith becomes more about our image or validation, it becomes less about love. And that loss of love, for God, and people, is what breaks the very core of our calling.

## Breaking the Grip of Self-Centered Faith

Self-centeredness is the greatest barrier to authentic community. When relationships are built on self-interest, they become transactional rather than transformational. But God designed us for something greater, Christ-centered relationships, sacrificial love, and a life that looks beyond ourselves.

The challenge is identifying the problem and asking, *What now?* How do we shift from a culture of self-centeredness to one of selflessness? The path forward is both about rejecting selfish habits and embracing new ones. This includes habits of sacrificial love, intentional connection, and a heart that prioritizes others over personal gain.

One powerful way to break free from self-centeredness is by intentionally serving those around us. Service pulls our focus outward, breaking the cycle of inward thinking and fostering a deeper sense of compassion. It doesn't have to be complicated. It can be as simple as reaching out to a friend, volunteering at a local shelter, or offering a listening ear to someone in need. When we make others a priority, we not only impact their lives but also experience transformation on our own. This isn't about diminishing our worth; it's about learning to think of ourselves less and love others more.

This shift in focus also invites us into deeper dependence on God. In a world that constantly tells us, *"You're enough on your own,"* selflessness teaches us that true fulfillment comes from trusting Him and loving others. As we embrace a life of service, we begin to see that real joy isn't found in what we achieve or acquire but in what we give. It's a paradox of the Kingdom: the more we pour out, the more we're filled.

We've already touched on how a self-focused culture has shaped our approach to relationships, often reducing them to transactions or performances. As we saw in Chapter 1, this relentless pursuit of personal success has created a society where connection is secondary to convenience. But here's the good news: we don't have to stay stuck in this cycle. We can choose to live differently, to reject the world's values and instead root ourselves in the selflessness of Christ.

> *real joy isn't found in what we achieve or acquire but in what we give.*

Unfortunately, the self-focused way of thinking has crept inside the church doors. Too often, we treat church as a service designed to meet our needs rather than a family to which we belong. And when the church adopts a transactional mindset, it risks losing its true identity. When church culture is shaped by convenience and consumption, community becomes something to attend or use, rather than a family to grow with and belong to.

It mirrors the societal trend of prioritizing efficiency and productivity over empathy and relationships. The result? Communities feel more like organizations, and people within them feel unseen and disconnected.

Throughout history, God has reminded His people that activity without a relationship misses the point entirely. The church was never meant to reflect the values of the world; it was created to reflect the heart of God's kingdom—a place where people matter more than programs and where love outweighs performance.

That's what this chapter is about: breaking free from the grip of self-centeredness and learning to love as Jesus did. His life wasn't about gaining recognition or applause; it was about serving others, even when it came at the highest cost. A "what's in it for me" attitude will always leave us feeling empty, but when we step into sacrificial love and service, something extraordinary happens.

We grow, the people around us are blessed, and the church becomes what it was always meant to be. So, let's take a look at what it means to stop focusing on ourselves and embrace the freedom, joy, and purpose that come from serving others, just like Christ did.

## Embracing Selflessness in a Self-Centered World

Selflessness is a bold and countercultural idea in a world that glorifies self-promotion and individualism. Everywhere we look, we're bombarded with messages urging us to prioritize ourselves, our needs, our ambitions, and the image we present to the world. Social media reinforcing the idea that success hinges on how well we showcase our lives. Career aspirations often revolve around climbing the corporate ladder, building a name for ourselves, and gaining recognition.

The message couldn't be clearer: life is all about *you*. But Jesus completely flips that narrative. He didn't just teach about selflessness; He modeled it with every action. He showed that true greatness isn't found in elevating ourselves but in serving others. As He said, *"The greatest among you will be your servant"* (Matthew 23:11). Through His life, Jesus redefined what it means to live with purpose and significance, demonstrating that fulfillment comes not from taking but from giving.

The challenge with selflessness is that it demands something uncomfortable. It's an inspiring concept, a lifestyle that requires humility and intentionality. Living selflessly means choosing to prioritize others above our desires, ambitions, and even our comfort.

When we focus less on self, we reflect more of Christ. His love wasn't passive or conditional. It was active, sacrificial, and deeply personal. And when we begin to live this way, we experience a shift in perspective. Instead of seeing people as obstacles to our success, we begin to see them as God does, worthy of love, grace, and compassion.

Philippians 2:3-4 says it perfectly: *"Do nothing out of selfish ambition or vain conceit. Rather, in humility value others above yourselves, not looking to your own interests but each of you to the interests of the others."*

Let those words sink in—*do nothing out of selfish ambition.* This isn't merely a suggestion or an ideal to strive for; it's a call to action, rooted in the very essence of Christ's character. When we embrace humility, we begin to mirror His heart, seeing the people around us not as competitors, but as individuals deeply deserving of our care and attention.

And here's the incredible part: when we take that brave step of shifting our focus outward, something transformative happens. Selflessness opens doors we didn't even know were closed. It deepens our relationships, fosters greater empathy, and helps us connect with others on a more meaningful level.

It strengthens the bonds within our communities, creating unity and purpose in ways that self-centeredness never could. Selflessness changes how we see the world. It moves us from a mindset of scarcity, constantly asking, *What can I get?*, to a God-centered perspective of abundance, joyfully asking, *What can I give?*

Here's the beautiful irony: when we live selflessly, we often find ourselves receiving blessings far beyond what we could have imagined. True selflessness isn't about losing—it's about gaining a life rich in love, connection, and purpose. It's discovering that when we give freely and wholeheartedly to others, we're filled with the very best that life has to offer. Selflessness invites us into a life of abundance, where giving becomes the key to truly living.

## Losing Our First Love

In Revelation 2:1-5, we come across a striking letter to the church of Ephesus, a community with an impressive legacy. Ephesus was a central hub of the early Christian movement. Founded by the Apostle Paul, pastored by Timothy, and later led by John the Apostle, this church had all the markings of spiritual vibrancy. They were deeply rooted in sound doctrine, rigorous theology, and a commitment to good works.

This was a church that worked tirelessly, demonstrated extraordinary patience, and remained steadfast in the face of challenges. On the surface, they seemed to be doing everything right. Yet, despite their commendable efforts, Jesus delivered a sobering message: *"You have abandoned the love you had at first"* (Revelation 2:4).

The Ephesian church had become a powerhouse of activity, defending truth, serving faithfully, and upholding God's name. But amidst all this busyness, something vital had been lost. They had drifted from their first love. At first glance, it seems like Jesus was highlighting their waning passion for Him, and while that was true, the issue ran deeper. They had not only lost their love for God but also their love for people.

The heart of the gospel, loving God and loving others, had been overshadowed by their relentless focus on doing church rather than *being* the church. They became so consumed with defending theology and running programs that they lost sight of their relational calling.

Jesus wasn't criticizing their dedication or hard work; He was inviting them to remember the *why* behind it all. The church was never meant to be a well-oiled machine of rituals, schedules, and appearances. It was designed to be a vibrant, living expression of Christ's love—a place where people could experience the grace, compassion, and truth of God in a real and transformative way.

The Ephesians had all the outward signs of success, but they had lost the relational heartbeat that breathes life into a church. Their story invites us to reflect and ask ourselves some tough questions: Are we merely going through the motions of faith? Are we so focused on working *for* God that we've forgotten to love *like* God?

If we're not careful, we can fall into the same trap, prioritizing tasks over people, and routines over relationships. When we stop measuring our worth by our performance and start leaning into the love of Christ, we rediscover the joy and freedom of a faith that is deeply relational.

Rekindling our first love isn't about adding more to our spiritual to-do list; it's about returning to the joy and simplicity of loving God and loving others. It means pausing the busyness to reconnect with the essence of the gospel: embodying Christ's love in every interaction.

This love, raw, honest, and relational, is what truly transforms our lives and the world around us. When we rediscover that first love, it reignites our purpose and reminds us why we began this journey of faith in the first place.

## The Love We Left Behind

God's perspective often turns our human understanding upside down. What we see as weakness, He calls strength. What the world dismisses as insignificant, God sees as purposeful. When the world says, "You're going down," God says, "You're rising up." Jesus emphasized this in one of His most countercultural teachings: *"The last shall be first, and the first shall be last."* While the world may label you as unqualified or unworthy, God declares the opposite.

He says, "You are chosen, capable, and fully equipped for My plans." The contrast couldn't be clearer—while the world values people for what they can offer, God values us for who we are and calls us to something infinitely greater.

The popular phrase *"It's not personal, it's business"* is often used to justify decisions that prioritize results over relationships, dismissing the need for compassion. But in God's kingdom, everything is personal. His way is all about relationships, love, and sacrificial care for others. Yet, it's so easy to get swept up in the world's narrative. We live in a culture that constantly pushes us to pursue success, self-reliance, and personal happiness, often at the expense of deeper connections.

These cultural messages are so deeply ingrained that they influence us in ways we may not even notice. That's why Paul's instruction in Romans 12:2 is vital: *"Do not conform to the pattern of this world."* As followers of Christ, we're called to a higher standard, yet the pull to conform can feel overwhelming. Whether it's through subtle pressures or outright expectations, the world constantly tries to shape us into its mold.

The reality is, we're shaped by what we consume; and today, consumption is constant. From social media feeds to advertisements, the messages are relentless: your worth is tied to your image, your possessions, and your achievements. Over time, this mindset begins to infiltrate our faith, distorting what it means to follow Jesus.

Instead of seeking God's will, we chase worldly success. Instead of investing in relationships, we build platforms and seek recognition. In many churches today, success is often measured by numbers, attendance, budgets, followers, rather than by spiritual depth, transformed lives, and authentic community. The focus shifts from substance to appearance, and we risk losing sight of what truly matters.

The consequences of this cultural drift are significant. On a personal level, prioritizing worldly values over God's leads to spiritual stagnation. When we pursue success, status, or self-image over intimacy with God, we lose touch with the source of true joy and fulfillment. This disconnect breeds emptiness, burnout, and even resentment.

Research from the Barna Group in 2022 found that people who focus solely on outward religious acts often experience higher levels of anxiety and less satisfaction than those who engage in authentic practices of faith. It's no surprise, faith that becomes routine and disconnected from genuine relationships will always leave us feeling hollow. God designed us for more.

The impact this has on the church is serious. When church culture becomes centered on consumption rather than genuine connection, its witness to the world weakens. People begin attending not to grow spiritually or build relationships but to be entertained or check a box. Programs and events take precedence, while the church's mission to disciple, love, and serve gets sidelined. Over time, this creates a passive congregation that watches rather than participates.

A consumer-driven church becomes more like a social club than a place of transformation, losing its ability to reflect the life-changing power of the gospel. When people outside the church see Christians who act no differently than the rest of the world, prioritizing appearances over genuine faith, they naturally question the authenticity of what we claim to believe.

Brennan Manning captures this problem powerfully in *The Ragamuffin Gospel*: *"The greatest single cause of atheism in the world today is Christians who acknowledge Jesus with their lips, walk out the door, and deny Him by their lifestyle. That is what an unbelieving world simply finds unbelievable."*

When our faith becomes more about rituals than relationships, it loses its power—not just for us, but for those watching. We trade the vibrant, life-giving love of Christ for a checklist of spiritual tasks, and in doing so, we abandon our first love.

Jesus made it clear: love, not sophisticated programs, not perfect performances, not flawless appearances, is the defining mark of His followers. In John 13:34-35, He said, *"A new command I give you: Love one another. As I have loved you, so you must love one another. By this, everyone will know that you are my disciples, if you love one another."* Notice what He didn't say.

He didn't say people would know us by how many verses we can quote, how eloquently we preach, or how impressive our church events are. He said they'd recognize us by our love. But how often do we miss this?

Many churches today risk losing sight of this truth. We get so caught up in perfecting our programs and streamlining operations that we forget about the people those ministries are meant to serve. We pour energy into making everything look perfect while people walk in and out of our buildings feeling unseen, unheard, and unloved.

> *When our faith becomes more about rituals than relationships, it loses its power*

This is the very issue Jesus addressed with the church in Ephesus in Revelation 2:4: *"You have forsaken the love you had at first."* The Ephesians were doing all the right things outwardly but had lost the heart behind it all, their love for God and people. Without that love, all their efforts, no matter how impressive, were empty.

The church was never meant to be a place for passive consumption. It was designed to be a transformative community where God's love changes lives. Every interaction we have is an opportunity to reflect that love—not treating people as projects or tasks but as individuals made in the image of God. It's this kind of love, genuine and relational, that the world desperately needs to see in us. Anything less misses the mark entirely.

# Shifting from Transactions to Genuine Connections

The church isn't a business. The gospel isn't a product. Worship isn't a performance. And God isn't a means to an end. These are truths we know deep down, yet sometimes, the way we act and operate tells a different story. Too often, it's easy to slip into the mentality of treating our faith like a transaction.

We reduce relationships to exchanges, something more like a trade than the real, deep connection Jesus showed us. But Jesus never entered into relationships to get something out of them. He wasn't transactional. He was transformative.

When you look at Jesus' life, you see this over and over again. He didn't spend time with people because they had something to offer Him. He spent time with the broken, the outcasts, and the ones who had nothing. He sat with lepers, ate with tax collectors, defended the adulterers, and healed the ones no one else wanted to touch. Why? Because His love was never about what they could do for Him, it was about who they were. His love was unconditional, freely given, and full of compassion. He didn't heal the sick or feed the hungry to become popular. He did it because that's who He is, a God of love and mercy.

Think about how Jesus built relationships with His disciples. He didn't choose them because they were influential or powerful. They weren't the religious elite, scholars, or rulers. They were everyday people, fishermen, a tax collector, and others who seemed completely ordinary.

They didn't bring impressive résumés or worldly qualifications; they simply brought a willingness to follow Him. Even then, they stumbled and failed along the way. Take Peter, for instance. He was bold and passionate, but he still denied Jesus three times during the most critical moment—the night of Jesus' arrest. Peter's failure could have been the end of his story.

In that moment, he looked like the last person deserving of grace. But Jesus didn't give up on him. After the resurrection, Jesus intentionally sought Peter out to restore him. He reminded Peter of his purpose and demonstrated that love and grace are more powerful than failure (John 21:15-19). That relationship wasn't based on Peter's performance; it was based the kind of transformative love that changes everything.

But when we allow a self-serving or performance-based approach to creep into our relationships, it distorts everything. We start treating people like commodities. It's harmful on a personal level and damages the health and unity of the entire church. This results in the church becoming something it was never meant to be. Instead of feeling like a family, it starts to feel like a business.

When this happens, the church loses its heartbeat. It stops being a place where people find healing, belonging, and transformation. Instead, it becomes an empty shell, going through the motions but missing the heart of what it's called to be.

Jesus showed us a completely different way to live. His love was patient, forgiving, and selfless. He didn't just talk about it; He lived it. He walked with people, listened to their struggles, and met them right where they were. And He calls us to follow His example. In John 13:34, He said, *"A new command I give you: Love one another. As I have loved you, so you must love one another."*

This command isn't about loving others when it's convenient or when it benefits us. It's about loving as Jesus loved, freely, sacrificially, and unconditionally. That's the kind of love that transforms not only relationships but entire communities.

A powerful example of this is Jesus washing His disciples' feet in John 13:3-17.

Despite being their Teacher and Lord, Jesus took on the role of a servant, kneeling down to wash the feet of those who followed Him, including Judas, who would soon betray Him. This act was a radical demonstration of humility, selflessness, and unconditional love. He didn't serve them out of obligation or for recognition. He did it to show them what real love looks like.

If we approach faith with a transactional lens, we miss out on the deeper joy of following Jesus. A self-focused faith is centered on what we can get, blessings, success, and recognition. But a faith rooted in love and service flips that perspective.

C.S. Lewis captures this beautifully in *Mere Christianity*: "Do not waste time bothering whether you 'love' your neighbor; act as if you did. As soon as we do this, we find one of the great secrets. When you are behaving as if you loved someone, you will presently come to love him." This is the power of choosing to love.

Love begins when we stop waiting for perfection and start stepping forward with intention and courage. When we choose to love, even when it's difficult, we reflect God's heart to the people around us. Love becomes the bridge that connects heaven's purpose to the world's needs.

As followers of Jesus, we're called to reject any idea that treats faith like a checklist or a transaction. Our relationship with God, and with others, isn't about what we can get out of it. It's about living in a way that shows the world who Jesus really is—the Savior who came not to be served but to serve and to give His life for everyone. When we embrace that kind of selfless love, we step into the fullness of the gospel, becoming living testimonies of the transformative power of grace.

## The Heart of the Gospel

At the heart of the gospel is the ultimate display of sacrificial love: Jesus laying down His life for us. John 15:13 puts it simply: *"Greater love has no one than this: to lay down one's life for one's friends."* This kind of love comes with a cost. But it's exactly the kind of love that Jesus calls us to extend to one another.

Sacrificial love is about stepping beyond what's comfortable or fits neatly into our plans. It asks us to willingly inconvenience ourselves for the sake of someone else. It's about showing up in the messiness of life, even when it's uncomfortable or untimely. It's choosing forgiveness instead of holding onto bitterness, generosity instead of selfishness, and compassion instead of judgment. In a culture that often glorifies self-preservation and personal gain, this kind of love shines as a powerful testament to the reality of Christ.

This love isn't an occasional act; it's essential for anyone who follows Jesus. It's the type of love that doesn't stop to count the cost but willingly pays the price because the reward, a life transformed by love, is so much greater. Sacrificial love impacts the people around us, but at the same time, it changes us too. It molds our character, deepens our faith, and aligns our hearts with the heart of God. It's through this love that we become more like Christ and discover the fullness of joy He intended for us.

The church was designed to be a living, breathing community where Christ's love is actively displayed in how we relate to one another. The early church modeled this beautifully. In Acts 2:42-47, we see a vivid picture of what relational living looks like: *"They devoted themselves to the apostles' teaching and to fellowship, to the breaking of bread and to prayer... They sold property and possessions to give to anyone who had need."* This wasn't a casual gathering or a group of people simply attending services. It was a family deeply committed to caring for one another and meeting each other's needs.

Relational living challenges us to move beyond surface-level interactions. It's not enough to smile at someone on Sunday morning or exchange pleasantries at a church potluck. Relational living calls us to invest in one another's lives; sharing burdens, celebrating victories, and walking together through life's highs and lows. It requires time, energy, and intentionality to truly love and care for the people God has placed around us.

True community doesn't happen by accident. It's built through consistent, intentional practices that reflect the heart of Christ. Gratitude keeps our hearts soft toward one another. Truth-telling creates trust and transparency. Hospitality opens the door for belonging, and keeping our promises shows that we're committed for the long haul.

These may seem like small things, but they're the very practices that turn a group of people into a spiritual family. When a church leans into these rhythms, it becomes a place where healing flows, growth is nurtured, and lives are continually transformed.

When the church embodies relational living, it becomes so much more than a place people attend, it becomes a refuge, a home, and a family. It becomes a haven for the broken, a place of belonging for the lonely, and a source of hope for the lost. Relational living is how we live out the command to "love your neighbor as yourself." It's how we answer Jesus' prayer in John 17:21, where He asked that we would be united, just as He and the Father are one. True unity doesn't come from events or strategies; it comes from relationships built on love, trust, and mutual respect.

Of course, relational living isn't without its challenges. It requires vulnerability, a willingness to open our lives to others and let them in. It

> *True unity doesn't come from events or strategies; it comes from relationships built on love, trust, and mutual respect.*

asks us to set aside our pride, our schedules, and even our personal preferences to prioritize the needs of others. It can be messy and uncomfortable at times, but the rewards are immeasurable. When we invest in authentic relationships, we tangibly reflect God's heart, drawing people closer to Him through the love we show. And in doing so, we become the church He designed us to be, a living testament to His transformative, sacrificial love.

## When Love is Needed Most

Nine years ago, my wife and I faced one of the most heart-wrenching experiences of our lives. We were expecting our second child, and life was full of joy and anticipation. The excitement was palpable as we looked forward to the weekend's doctor appointment, where we'd find out our baby's gender—a moment we had dreamed of celebrating together. After the appointment, we had plans to leave on a cruise, a special trip to celebrate the joy of our growing family.

The morning of the appointment began like any other. We walked into the doctor's office, chatting about our guesses for the baby's gender. The nurse came in, cheerful and talkative, and began the sonogram. Her lighthearted demeanor gave no hint of what was to come. But as she moved the wand across my wife's belly, her expression shifted. Her smile faded into something more serious. She glanced at us briefly before asking, "When was your last appointment?"

Confused, I answered, "Three weeks ago. Everything was fine then. Why?" She hesitated, brushing off my question with a vague, "Just checking," but her worried face betrayed her attempt to remain calm. The room fell into a heavy silence as she focused intently on the screen. Moments later, she excused herself and came back with the doctor.

The tension in the room was palpable. The doctor asked the same question: "When was your last appointment?" My heart began to race, and a knot formed in my stomach. "Three weeks ago," I repeated, my voice now shaking. "Is something wrong?"

The doctor sighed, her face softening with compassion. "I'm so sorry," she said gently. "There is no heartbeat. We can't find a heartbeat."

Her words hit like a physical blow, shattering our world in an instant. My mind raced with disbelief. *No heartbeat? How could this be happening?* This wasn't how the day was supposed to go. We were supposed to be celebrating, not grieving. The doctor explained that my wife was too far along and would need to be induced to deliver the baby. "Go home, prepare yourselves, and come back," she advised gently. The drive home was excruciatingly quiet, the air in the car thick with grief. At home, my wife quietly packed her bag and showered while I sat, struggling to hold back tears and make sense of what was happening.

At the hospital, the induction of the labor process began, but my wife's body wasn't ready. She was only 20 weeks along. Watching her endure it was one of the most heart-wrenching experiences of my life. The nurses were kind and gentle, offering words of sympathy and apologizing often, but nothing they said could lift the unbearable weight of what was happening. After hours of labor, one nurse leaned in and spoke softly, "One more push." My wife, exhausted but determined, drew upon every ounce of strength she had left.

And then, there was silence. A silence so profound and heavy that it felt as if time itself had come to a halt. No cries. No joyful cheers. Just stillness, thick and unrelenting, stretching on endlessly.

The nurse gently placed the baby on my wife's chest, and silent tears began to stream down her face. Without a word, the nurse quietly stepped out, giving us a moment alone. We sat there in the stillness, holding each other and the weight of our loss. No words came; none felt adequate. In that heartbreaking silence, we wept together, overwhelmed by grief, so heavy that it felt impossible to carry. It was a moment no one could truly prepare for, one that left us clinging to each other as the reality of our pain settled deep in our souls.

I'll never forget leaving the hospital. I pushed my wife in a wheelchair toward the exit, her face pale, her eyes hollow. Resting in her lap was a small box the size of a shoebox. In it, a painful, quiet reminder of the life and memories we would never get to share. Each step toward the car felt heavier than the last, like the world itself was pressing in on us. That small box held more than just keepsakes; it carried the weight of shattered dreams and a future that had disappeared before it even began.

As we were driving back home, I understood something that has stayed with me ever since. As I wrestled with the agony of the loss and after all we had gone through in the last 24 hours, the last thing I wanted at that moment was an elegant sermon, a powerful worship song, or an expertly organized church program.

As meaningful as those things can be, there is no way, they couldn't reach the depths of the pain my wife and I were feeling in that moment. We didn't need theology explained, we needed love expressed. We needed the kind of selfless love that doesn't try to fix the pain but chooses to carry it with you. What we needed most wasn't words or answers, it was presence. We needed someone to sit with us in the silence, to hold us, and to simply say, "I'm here. You're not alone."

# Chapter 4
# The Ministry of Presence

Through the experience of losing a child, I learned that the most powerful ministry doesn't come from eloquent speeches or perfect solutions. It comes from the quiet, simple act of showing up. Sometimes, showing up speaks louder than a thousand words.

In life's darkest, heaviest moments, when the pain feels unbearable, presence matters more than words or actions. Just being there speaks love. It's about standing alongside someone in their grief and reminding them that they don't have to carry it alone. That kind of love, the kind that simply shows up, is what heals. It's the kind of love that reflects the very heart of God.

For me, this life-changing event left me wrestling with questions that had always lingered beneath the surface. What does it really mean to live out the gospel, not just at church, but in the ordinary, everyday rhythm of life? That question became a turning point for me, pushing me to look beyond the routines of religion and into something far deeper.

Growing up in church, everything seemed centered around getting the religious part right. We focused on following the rules and planning our Sunday mornings down to the smallest detail. It was about "doing church" the right way, and every moment was accounted for. But as the years passed, I always felt that something was missing.

We had taken an infinite, all-powerful God and tried to fit Him into boxes we could understand and control. It's like we had made Him small, turning a limitless God into something manageable. While the intentions were good, religion has a way of putting boundaries around God's mystery, leaving little room for the fullness of who He is. The structures we set up to manage the move of God became the very barriers that prevented Him from continuing to move in our lives.

But God was never meant to fit inside our boxes. Slowly and gently, He began challenging the way I saw Him and the routines I had tied to my faith. Worship started to mean more than just singing songs on Sundays. Justice—God's heart for making things right, defending the vulnerable, and standing for those in need—transformed from an abstract idea into something deeply personal, and representing Him became about so much more than simply attending church services.

Even the scriptures I'd memorized as a kid, verses I thought I'd mastered, suddenly felt alive, carrying a new weight as if they were speaking directly to the tension in my heart. It was clear: God was calling me to step deeper, to let go of "performing" religion, and embrace a life where His presence is not only a part of my routine but also the foundation of everything.

## A Deeper Calling

What God wanted was not for me to check all the boxes or perform religious tasks perfectly. He was calling me to live in a way where His heart was reflected in every part of my life. It wasn't enough to know about Him; my life had to show His character. Standing for what is right, kindness, and presence became more than words, they became the foundation of what it means to live as His representative.

The ministry of presence started to take hold of my heart. This isn't about showing up with answers or fixing people's problems; it's about showing up with love, empathy, and a willingness to simply be there. In a world that values busyness and tasks over relationships, being fully present with others is revolutionary. It means slowing down, seeing people the way God sees them, and recognizing that every moment of connection can reflect His heart.

> *The ministry of presence turns ordinary moments into sacred ones.*

True hospitality isn't about planning social events or hosting polished gatherings. It's about creating a space where people feel safe, seen, and welcome. It's the kind of presence that goes beyond casual friendliness and steps into sacred ground. When we choose to slow down, listen deeply, and show up with compassion, we create moments where people can encounter the love of God through us. This is what it means to hold space for someone, to be fully present without judgment or distraction, offering a quiet strength that allows healing to begin.

As I began to live this out, I realized the gospel isn't necessarily in the big dramatic moments; it's in the small, everyday ones. It's the conversations over coffee, the quiet act of kindness to a stranger, or sitting with someone in their grief. Presence doesn't make headlines, but it's transformative. Jesus modeled this throughout His ministry. He met people where they were, saw them for who they were, and made sure they knew they were loved.

This kind of life requires us to be vessels that are open to His calling, willing to reflect His heart, and ready to meet people where they are. The ministry of presence turns ordinary moments into sacred ones. It's not flashy or loud, but it's deeply meaningful. The more I lean into this calling, the more I see how God works in those small, unassuming moments. That's where His heart is most powerfully revealed, and that's where transformation begins.

## The Crisis of Religion Without Presence

When religion loses sight of justice, the call to uphold righteousness, defend the vulnerable, and care for those in need, along with kindness, it completely misrepresents who God is. Instead of being this vibrant, life-changing force, faith can get reduced to empty routines that don't actually reflect His heart. You see this clearly in Isaiah 58:1-5. God doesn't call out His people for neglecting worship altogether. He confronts them about *how* they were worshiping.

On the outside, they seemed to have it all together. They were making the sacrifices, singing the songs, and following the rituals. But their lives didn't align with the heart of the God they claimed to honor. And God's response? It's sharp and impossible to ignore.

*"You worship as if you were those who practice justice and goodness, as if your life reflected My character. But you are absorbed with*

*yourselves, focused on your own interests, while neglecting the things that truly matter."*

God's words cut straight through the surface, exposing what's really going on. The people's worship had become disconnected from their lives. They were saying the right things and following the rituals, but their actions didn't reflect the heart of the God they claimed to serve. This was an issue for ancient Israel and something that we also wrestle with. It's all too easy to fall into the same trap, focusing on the outward expressions of worship while ignoring God's deeper call to justice, mercy, and showing up for others.

Here is the real question: what happens when all that effort to get things perfect with our services and programs overshadows what worship is truly about? If our worship doesn't change the way we live, how we treat people, how we respond to injustice, and how we show up for the hurting, then we've missed the whole point.

When we think about worship, it's easy to focus on what happens on Sundays, the songs, the sermons, the programs. But God's idea of worship is so much bigger than that. Worship is about how our time with Him changes the way we live. It's about stepping out of the sanctuary and into the lives of those who are hurting, being present with them, and reflecting His love in practical ways.

In Isaiah 58, God makes it clear that His definition of worship, more often than not, differs from ours. I'm not saying He doesn't care at all about how our worship sounds or looks—But I believe He cares more about how it changes us and impacts those around us.

God's questions are clear and challenging: Are you standing with the oppressed? Are you caring for those who are suffering?

Are you looking after the widows and orphans? Are justice, mercy, and kindness a part of your everyday life? This is what matters to Him.

Worship isn't a performance; it's about presence. God's presence living in us and our presence in the lives of those who need it most. True worship pulls us outward. It calls us to reflect God's heart in the places where it's needed most, in the lives of the hurting, the overlooked, and the marginalized.

Jesus talked about justice and mercy, and lived it. He touched the untouchable (*Matthew 8:2-3*), shared meals with sinners (*Luke 5:29-32*), and stood up for the oppressed (*Luke 4:18-19*). His life was a living reflection of Isaiah 58. A picture of what it means to embody God's heart for justice and goodness. As Isaiah 58:10 says, 'If you spend yourselves on behalf of the hungry and satisfy the needs of the oppressed, then your light will rise in the darkness, and your night will become like the noonday.'

When we leave justice and kindness out of our worship, it's not just an issue of what we do; it's an issue of who we are. We fail to reflect God's character, and we lose sight of our purpose as His representatives. This is why Isaiah's words still hit home today. They remind us that worship isn't about what happens in the sanctuary; it's about how we live every single day.

This same tension shows up over and over in scripture. We see it in Samuel's story, serving in the temple but not yet truly knowing the God he served. We see it in Jesus' confrontation with the Pharisees, who followed every religious rule but missed the heart of the law. And we see it here in Isaiah, where God makes it clear: He doesn't want our rituals; He wants our hearts. Worship that isn't rooted in justice, mercy, and love misses the point entirely.

## Justice and Kindness as Worship

When we hear the word *justice*, it's easy to picture courtrooms or a rigid sense of rules being enforced. But God's justice is so much bigger than that. God's justice doesn't revolve around punishment or rules. It brings restoration to what's been broken. It's stepping into the hard places, standing with those who've been pushed aside, and reaching out to the hurting with love.

This kind of justice can't exist without kindness, not just politeness, but a deep, intentional kindness that flows straight from God's character. Together, justice and kindness become acts of worship, ways we reflect who God is in the way we live and love.

When Jesus walked among us, His ministry wasn't confined to words or sermons. When He reached out to lepers, people who were shunned and isolated by society, He didn't just heal them with a word, He physically touched them.

That was a radical act, because according to Jewish law, touching a leper made you unclean. No one dared to come that close. But Jesus did. His touch wasn't just about healing their bodies; it was about breaking the barrier of rejection and restoring their worth. He met them in the very place others refused to go.

Healing begins in spaces where people feel seen and valued. He ate with the outcasts, welcomed sinners, and gave hope to those the world had written off. Everything He did pointed back to the heart of God—a heart that values restoration, compassion, and presence. Jesus' life was the ultimate example of worship lived out through justice and kindness.

The connection between justice, kindness, and worship is a thread that runs throughout Scripture. Micah 6:8 sums it up perfectly: "He has shown you, O mortal, what is good. And what does the

Lord require of you? To act justly and to love mercy and to walk humbly with your God."

Justice is about stepping in where there's brokenness and making things right. Mercy is forgiveness; it's literally love in action. And humility? It's walking closely with God, letting His heart guide everything we do.

For followers of Christ, justice and kindness aren't optional. They're central to what it means to live out our faith. Worship isn't confined to the songs we sing on Sunday mornings or the prayers we pray in church. When we step into the lives of the marginalized, the oppressed, and the forgotten, we're worshiping God in the most genuine way possible. We're showing the world His heart, His love, and His presence.

Justice and kindness often come with a cost. They ask us to step out of our comfort zones, and sacrifice our time, energy, and resources for the sake of others. When we choose to live this way, we align ourselves with God's purpose, becoming part of something far bigger than ourselves. Justice and kindness are more than just good deeds—they're worship in its truest form. They're the way we show the world who God is, reflecting His heart in everything we do.

## The Call to Reflect God's Character

Jesus' life was a perfect example of what it looks like to reflect the heart of God. He talked about love, justice, and compassion and lived them out in every interaction. In Matthew 25:35-40, Jesus paints a vivid picture of what it means to truly embody His character. He talks about feeding the hungry, clothing the naked, visiting the sick, and welcoming the stranger.

These aren't grand, unattainable gestures; they're small, everyday actions. But in their simplicity, they carry eternal significance. Jesus' words are clear: "Whatever you did for one of the least of these brothers and sisters of mine, you did for me."

That statement is profound and deeply challenging. He makes a direct connection between how we treat others and how we treat Him. It's not about putting on a show of religious devotion or impressing others with outward acts of faith. Instead, it's about being present for the people who are often overlooked, the hungry, the lonely, the marginalized. To us, these acts might seem small, like feeding someone or visiting someone in need. But to God, they are acts of worship, a reflection of His heart that speaks louder than any sermon or song ever could.

The problem is, it's easy to get caught up in what some might call spiritual overindulgence. We dive deep into theology, spending hours dissecting scripture and expanding our knowledge, but we fail to let that understanding move us to action. We perfect our Sunday services, making sure the music, lighting, and every detail is flawless, yet outside those walls, the widows and orphans remain forgotten, and the oppressed remain unseen. This is not the gospel Jesus lived. Unfortunately, some of us get so caught up in getting our Sunday's right that we forget to get our life right.

Living out the gospel requires us to challenge our own comfort and routines. Stepping into situations that disrupt our schedules or stretch us in ways that aren't convenient. But that's what Jesus calls us to do. He asks us to let go of our self-focused priorities and embrace a life of love that costs us something. These actions change lives, both for those we serve and for us.

The passage in Matthew 25 isn't meant to be a checklist of good deeds; it's a guide for living a life that mirrors God's heart. Every encounter with someone in need is an opportunity to show them God's love. When we feed someone, it's more than giving them food, we're reminding them that they are loved. When we welcome someone, we create a space where they can belong.

In a culture that glorifies achievement and self-promotion, Jesus' call to reflect God's character is countercultural. It shifts the focus from personal success to selfless service, from seeking recognition to building relationships. It moves us from platform ministries to quiet faithfulness, where the goal isn't to be seen by crowds, but to be known by God and to truly know others. This way of living out the gospel requires us to trade status for servanthood. It's not always easy, but in those moments of sacrifice, we come closest to understanding the heart of God.

> *Being present for others is one of the most powerful ways we can reflect God's heart.*

Theologian N.T. Wright captures this beautifully in *Simply Christian* when he writes, "When we look after the poor, we are quite literally meeting Jesus in them. We are joining Him in His mission to restore the world, one act of love at a time." This perspective changes everything. Serving others is about joining Jesus in His work of restoration. Every meal shared, every kind word offered, and every moment spent with someone in need becomes holy. It's a chance for heaven to touch the earth.

Being present for others is one of the most powerful ways we can reflect God's heart. It doesn't require expertise or a platform; it requires compassion, humility, and a willingness to step into the messy realities of life. When we live this way, we become living testimonies of God's love. We bring hope to the hopeless, light to the darkness, and show the world what it means to truly follow Jesus.

We live in a culture where relationships are reduced to quick texts and quick interactions. But Jesus calls us to something entirely different. He calls us to slow down, to truly see the people around us, and to step into their lives with intention. It means putting aside our to-do lists and agendas to be fully present with the people who need us. It's crazy to say, but in a world where efficiency often takes priority over empathy, this kind of presence feels radical.

Paul captures this beautifully in Galatians 6:2: *"Carry each other's burdens, and in this way you will fulfill the law of Christ."* That law isn't about achieving something great; it's about walking with others through life, reflecting God's love as we do.

## The Importance of Empathy and Understanding in Relationships

Empathy and understanding are the cornerstones of valuable relationships. They allow us to connect with others on a deeper level, moving beyond surface interactions to truly see and value the person in front of us. Jesus modeled this beautifully throughout His ministry, whether it was stopping to heal the blind man (Mark 10:46-52), weeping with Mary and Martha over the loss of Lazarus (John 11:35), or washing the feet of His disciples (John 13:12-17).

In each instance, He demonstrated a willingness to step into the experiences and emotions of others, meeting them where they were with compassion and care. Empathy is an intentional act of love that reflects God's heart for His people.

To develop empathy, we need to cultivate active listening. This means being fully present when someone is speaking, not just waiting for our turn to talk. James 1:19 encourages us to *"be quick to listen, slow to speak, and slow to become angry"*. Practically, this might involve setting aside distractions, like putting down our phones, maintaining eye contact, and asking thoughtful questions to clarify what someone is sharing. Active listening is a skill that helps us understand what someone is saying and what they're feeling beneath the surface. It communicates that we value their perspective, even if we don't fully agree with it.

Another way to build empathy is by intentionally broadening our perspective. Reading diverse stories, engaging with people from different backgrounds, and practicing the art of curiosity can help us step outside our own experiences. Jesus exemplified this in how He engaged with people who were often marginalized by society, like the Samaritan woman at the well (John 4:1-26) or Zacchaeus, the tax collector (Luke 19:1-10). He didn't avoid these interactions; He sought them out, showing us that understanding others requires stepping into their world and seeing life through their eyes. Empathy grows when we're willing to move beyond assumptions and truly seek to understand.

Prayer is another powerful tool for fostering empathy. When we pray for others, especially those we struggle to understand, God softens our hearts and aligns them with His. Philippians 2:3-5 reminds us to *"value others above yourselves, not looking to your own interests but each of you to the interests of*

> *The gospel was never intended to be a product to market or consume.*

*the others. In your relationships with one another, have the same mindset as Christ Jesus".*

Practical strategies include praying for God to help us see others as He sees them and to respond to their needs with His love and grace. Empathy isn't about always having the perfect response; it's about showing up, being present, and reflecting the compassionate heart of Christ in every interaction.

## Reclaiming the Church's Identity

At its core, the church was designed to be a close-knit community of people fully committed to reflecting God's love in every part of their lives. The church is meant to be a living, breathing expression of God's heart. But somewhere along the way, cultural pressures and worldly standards crept in and began to redefine its purpose, and the church's true identity became blurred. This has caused some to lose sight of the church's sacred calling. The gospel was never intended to be a product to market or consume. It's meant to be lived, shared, and experienced.

When we think about a real community, it's easy to picture a perfect group of people who always get along, always help each other, and never struggle. But let's be honest, community is messy. Real community doesn't depend on flawless connection. It grows when we choose to show up in life's hard moments. It's not helping out when it's convenient or easy. It's stepping into someone else's struggle and saying, "You don't have to carry this alone." It's sharing the weight, being present, and reminding them they're not forgotten. This is love in action, the kind of love that shows the heart of Jesus more powerfully than words ever could.

The ministry of presence is about being willing to walk alongside others, through the ups and the downs, and letting them know they're seen, loved, and never alone. Unfortunately, most people won't slow down long enough to truly invest in someone else's life—unless they see a personal benefit. But when we choose to carry each other's burdens, we fulfill the law of Christ, not by doing something extraordinary but by simply being there for each other.

What would happen if we focused less on perfecting our programs and more on fostering meaningful relationships? The simplicity and authenticity of the early church challenge us to rethink our priorities. What if our best "strategy" for reaching people was simply loving each other well?

That kind of love, the love Jesus described in John 13:35 when He said, *"By this everyone will know that you are my disciples, if you love one another"*, is both powerful and radically different from the world's way of living. The early Christian movement talked about love but they also made sure they lived it. Their love was both expressed in words and demonstrated through sacrificial acts of kindness and presence.

When we reclaim the church's identity as a family, the church becomes a community where brokenness is healed, where the lonely find belonging, and where the weary are renewed. It becomes a sanctuary of grace and a living reflection of God's unconditional love. But rediscovering this identity takes intentionality. It requires us to move away from the perspective that treats the church as a provider of spiritual goods and services.

Francis Chan picks up on this in *Letters to the Church* when he challenges the way many modern churches operate. He writes, "We've created systems that keep people busy but rarely connect them in a significant way." This is difficult to admit, but there is so much truth in that statement. It's easy to fill our calendars with events, but are we really building relationships? Are we creating spaces where people feel like they truly belong, or are we just giving them more things to do?

Here's the challenge: How are we, as individuals and as a church, creating that kind of community? What steps can we take to move beyond surface-level interactions and into relationships that reflect God's heart? We need to be a church that doesn't just open its doors but opens its arms, walking with people through every high and low. Because, in the end, that's what genuine belonging looks like. God's love in action, one relationship at a time.

Reclaiming the church's identity also means recognizing that every single person has a role to play. The church isn't only the responsibility of pastors or leaders; it belongs to everyone who calls it home. In 1 Corinthians 12, Paul describes the church as a body made up of many parts, each uniquely gifted and essential to the whole. When every part of the body functions as it should, the church thrives. Its collective impact becomes something truly extraordinary. As followers of Christ, our lives should be marked by justice, kindness, and presence. These aren't optional extras, they're central to our calling.

## Action through Presence

The truth is that the most impactful sermons aren't the ones preached from pulpits, they're the ones lived out in the ordinary, everyday moments of our lives. True ministry happens in hospital waiting rooms, around kitchen tables, and on sidewalks where tears fall. It happens when we choose to show up for people in the moments that matter most.

Being present is how we remind others of God's presence. Christine Pohl writes in *Living into Community*, "The witness of a shared life speaks louder than any words." Our presence, when offered with love and humility, becomes a powerful testimony of God's grace. It tells the grieving they're not alone, assures the oppressed that they're seen, and reminds the hopeless that light still exists.

But the Ministry of Presence isn't without its challenges. It requires sacrifice. It calls us to listen more than we speak, to sit in silence when words fail, and to give of ourselves without expecting anything in return. This kind of ministry can be emotionally draining, but it's also deeply rewarding. Every time we show up for others, we're joining in God's redemptive work. We're letting His love shine through our actions, reminding people of His presence in their lives.

In a world obsessed with busyness, the Ministry of Presence invites us to slow down and value relationships over productivity. James 1:27 highlights that true religion involves caring for those in distress, reminding us that service and presence are central to our faith.

Helping others and being transformed in the process go hand in hand. As we reflect God's heart through acts of love and justice, we experience His presence more deeply in our own lives. In showing up for others, we reflect a God who is always present, profoundly loving, and deeply invested in His people.

This is an invitation to transformation and a call to action. When we embrace the ministry of presence, we find that our own lives are changed in the process. We see God's heart more clearly, experience His love more deeply, and discover the joy of living a life rooted in service. As stated before, the Ministry of Presence isn't about fixing problems or having all the answers. It's about reflecting the God we serve. A God who is always present, always loving, and always faithful.

# Chapter 5
# Breaking Barriers to Connection

Feeling disconnected can happen even in the most welcoming environments. A pastor's wife once shared, "People think I have a perfect life because I'm the pastor's wife, but sometimes I sit in the back of the sanctuary and wonder, does anyone see me?" Another young man said, "I've been in a small group for months, but I still feel like an outsider. It's like they already have their circle, and I'm just on the edge." These stories show how common it is to feel disconnected, even in a place where we're supposed to find a connection.

Even as we aim to connect, the pace of life often gets in the way. Whether it's through technology or packed schedules, we rush past the moments that could draw us closer together. Technology gives us ways to communicate, but it can leave our relationships feeling shallow. We scroll through social media, leave a quick comment or a like, and convince ourselves we've connected. But have we really? Even in the church, these habits show up. We text instead of calling, email instead of meeting, and wonder why we still feel distant.

Disconnection can also creep into the most unexpected places. We might be busy serving, attending every event, or even leading ministries, yet we still feel like something is missing. What matters most isn't the amount of activity, but the depth of connection we build along the way.

When we look at Jesus, we see a different way. He faced the same kinds of barriers in His ministry, like when He met the Samaritan woman at the well (John 4). Her community avoided her because of her past, but Jesus didn't see her mistakes or her reputation. He saw her heart. He listened to her and showed her grace. That one moment changed her life forever.

Jesus' example shows us what it takes to build real relationships. It means slowing down enough to put aside our plans and be willing to meet people where they are. For leaders, it might mean being vulnerable and modeling this kind of connection. For everyone else, it's about making room for people to feel seen, not as projects, but as part of God's family.

The truth is, these barriers, fear, busyness, cultural habits, are real, but they don't have to stop us. When we commit to loving people the way Jesus did, the church can become a deep-knit community.

## Confronting Relational Barriers

Building real relationships takes effort, and it's often the thing we struggle with the most. In the church, relational barriers come with unique challenges. Ministry life brings its pressures, and while we understand the value of connection, actually getting there can feel like hitting an invisible wall.

One of the biggest walls is fear. For church members, this might look like hesitating to join a small group or staying quiet during a tough season because you're afraid of being judged. For leaders, fear can take the form of hiding personal struggles to keep up an image of strength. A ministry leader once shared, "I feel like I'm walking a tightrope. If I share too much, I'm afraid people will lose respect for me." This kind of fear keeps us from being honest and stops us from building the relationships we need to thrive.

Another challenge is unresolved hurt. Whether it's a small misunderstanding or a bigger conflict, those wounds can linger and impact how we relate to others. In the church, where expectations are often higher, these hurts can feel especially heavy. One member shared with me how a minor disagreement over a ministry decision led to years of bitterness. "I didn't even realize how much I was holding onto until someone pointed it out," she said. Holding onto these hurts creates distance while at the same time stalling our spiritual growth.

Busyness is another major barrier. Leaders juggle sermons, programs, and pastoral care, while members manage work, family, and personal commitments. All this leaves little room for meaningful connection. Even within the church, relationships can get pushed aside by packed schedules. We do care, but when everything feels urgent, making time becomes a real challenge.

Technology and cultural individualism also contribute to disconnection. While digital tools make communication easier, they often lack the depth of face-to-face conversations. Similarly, the cultural emphasis on independence and self-reliance can make it hard to lean on others or let them in. These topics will be explored in depth later, but it's important to recognize how they create barriers to authentic connection.

Fear, unforgiveness, busyness, and cultural habits don't have to define our relationships. When we address these challenges with humility and intention, we create the kind of connection God designed us for.

## Fear and Insecurity

One of the biggest barriers to building heartfelt connections is fear. Fear of rejection, judgment, or being misunderstood can cause people to hold back and keep parts of themselves hidden. For church members, this might mean hesitating to share a prayer request because they're worried about what others might think. For leaders, it can mean staying silent about personal struggles to maintain the appearance of strength.

As a pastor or leader, you can feel like you're expected to have all the answers. And deep down, you might wonder, if you admit you're struggling, will people lose respect for you? This pressure to always appear strong often isolates leaders, cutting them off from the relationships they need to thrive. Vulnerability feels risky, something they can't afford to show. Over time, this unspoken expectation can lead to burnout, leaving leaders feeling disconnected and diminishing their ability to lead with authenticity and joy.

When leaders feel like they can't share their struggles, it also sends an unintended message to the congregation: that faith is about looking like you have it all together, rather than leaning on grace. By being open about their challenges, leaders strengthen their relationships and foster a church culture where honesty is celebrated over appearances. Vulnerability from the top creates ripples throughout the community, reminding everyone that it's okay to be human, lean on one another, and grow together in grace. This allows us to build bridges when we choose understanding over judgment.

## **Unforgiveness**

Unresolved conflict is one of the most challenging barriers to building relational depth. When someone hurts us, whether they meant to or not, it's natural to feel the sting of injustice. That initial pain can quickly turn into a wound we revisit over and over, replaying the situation in our minds.

In the church, where we often hold relationships to higher standards, these hurts can feel even sharper. We expect kindness, grace, and understanding, so when those expectations aren't met, the disappointment can turn into bitterness.

Unforgiveness not only affects the relationship where the hurt began, but it can spill over into other parts of our lives. Bitterness colors how we see people, situations, and even God. R.T. Kendall, in *Total Forgiveness*, calls unforgiveness "a prison of our own making." When we hold onto resentment, we block the work of the Holy Spirit and hinder our spiritual growth, leaving us trapped in cycles of pain and isolation.

Jesus made it clear that forgiveness is both urgent and essential. In Matthew 5:23-24, He teaches, *"If you are offering your gift at the altar and there remember that your brother or sister has something against you, leave your gift there in front of the altar. First, go and be reconciled to them; then come and offer your gift."* This passage shows that forgiveness is both about mending relationships with others and at the same time deeply tied to our relationship with God. When we let unresolved conflict linger, it creates barriers in both directions.

Forgiveness doesn't mean ignoring the hurt or pretending it didn't happen. It means making a choice to release the other person from the debt of their offense and trusting God to heal what's broken.

Lewis B. Smedes, in *Forgive and Forget: Healing the Hurts We Don't Deserve*, writes, "To forgive is to set a prisoner free and discover that the prisoner was you." Forgiveness doesn't excuse the hurt. It creates the space for you to break free from the bitterness that keeps you stuck. Only then can reconciliation and peace begin to take root.

The church is at its best when forgiveness is practiced openly and consistently. Both leaders and members need to create a culture where it's safe to admit mistakes and seek reconciliation. When conflict is handled with humility and grace, it reflects the heart of Christ and removes one of the biggest barriers to connection. This kind of intentional forgiveness allows relationships to heal and grow, transforming the church into a gospel-centered community of love and unity.

## Busyness

Being busy has basically become the norm for most of us. We wear it like it's something to be proud of, like a full calendar means we're doing something meaningful. But when that hustle mindset creeps into our church life, it starts to chip away at our relationships. We get so caught up in meetings, ministries, and managing everything that we forget to slow down, take a breath, and actually connect with the people around us.

For church leaders, it's easy to get so caught up in prepping sermons, leading teams, and planning events that your own spiritual health and relationships start to take a back seat. One leader put it perfectly: "It feels like I'm always pouring out, but no one's pouring back into me." That kind of nonstop rhythm can leave you drained and disconnected, even from the people who are supposed to help you stay grounded. And honestly, it's not just leaders. People in the congregation feel it too, trying to juggle work, school, family, and everything else. Before long, church starts to feel more like another box to check off than a place to build real, life-giving relationships.

> *Real relationships require time and attention*

John Mark Comer, in *The Ruthless Elimination of Hurry*, reminds us of the importance of slowing down, writing, "Hurry is incompatible with love." Real relationships require time and attention, two things busyness steals from us. When we pack our lives with programs and activities, even good ones, we risk crowding out opportunities for authentic fellowship.

The good news is that we can push back against the culture of busyness. By simplifying ministry schedules, encouraging smaller gatherings, and prioritizing unhurried fellowship, churches can create space for relationships to grow. These choices may seem small, but they open the door to deeper connections and a stronger sense of community.

Rest and relationships aren't luxuries—they're essentials. When we make space for the pauses that allow relationships to flourish, we honor God's design for community. Relationships don't grow in the rush; they grow in the moments where we slow down, look each other in the eye, and share life.

## Digital Disconnection

Digital technology has completely changed how we communicate, making it easier to stay in touch but harder to connect deeply. A quick text or a social media comment might feel like an interaction, but these exchanges often lack the empathy and presence needed for true relationships. In church life, this can make connections feel more transactional than transformational, leaving people feeling unseen even when they seem engaged.

Scrolling through social media can give us updates on people's lives, but it rarely tells the full story. The pressure to present an idealized version of ourselves often leads to surface-level interactions. Instead of fostering vulnerability, these curated realities can create a sense of isolation, as if everyone else has it all together while we struggle in silence. This dynamic can keep real issues hidden, even in spaces meant for authenticity.

Henry Cloud and John Townsend, in their book *Boundaries*, remind us, "We can't grow closer to others without being real." For the church, this means creating spaces where people feel safe to let their guard down. These are places where conversations go beyond emojis and likes to deeper, life-giving connections.

Technology is a great tool for staying in touch, but it can never take the place of a real, face-to-face connection. There's something irreplaceable about sitting across from someone, sharing a moment, and truly being present. Small groups, personal check-ins, and worshiping together create the kind of deep, authentic relationships that a screen just can't replicate.

As churches step into the digital age, the goal is to use technology with wisdom, ensuring that it supports real community instead of replacing it. At the end of the day, what feels like distance can actually become a doorway for God's grace to draw us closer.

## Cultural Individualism

Our culture celebrates independence and self-reliance, but these values come at a cost. While they drive ambition and achievement, they also isolate us, both in our daily lives and within the church. We're so used to chasing our own goals that we don't leave much space for the kind of healthy dependence on each other that God actually designed us for.

In church, this kind of mindset can show up as a "me-first" approach to faith. People come looking for a boost, some encouragement, a message that speaks to them, and there's nothing wrong with that. But sometimes, we forget to ask, *"How can I show up for someone else today?"* When that happens, church starts to feel more like a place we go to *get something* instead of a family we belong to, a group of people doing life together, not just attending the same service.

Dietrich Bonhoeffer, in his book *Life Together*, offers a powerful reminder: "The person who loves their dream of community will destroy community, but the person who loves those around them will create community." His words challenge us to move beyond idealized visions of connection and instead invest in the people right in front of us. Christ-centered connection isn't about perfection; it's about commitment.

To push back against the pull toward isolation, the church has to be really intentional about creating a sense of shared purpose and belonging. Things like serving together, sharing meals, and having real conversations about how much we actually need each other, that's what helps reshape what it means to be part of the body of Christ. When we live with that kind of unity, it strengthens our relationships and shows the world that deep, meaningful connection is possible.

## Biblical Perspective

To overcome the barriers that divide us, we have to go back to the foundation of Scripture. Jesus' teachings and the apostolic letters give us a clear path toward authentic connection. In Matthew 5:23-24, Jesus reminds us just how important reconciliation is to God. He tells us that before we come to worship, before we even bring our gifts to the altar, we must first make peace with those we've wronged or those who have wronged us. This shows us that broken relationships affect our connection with others and disrupt our communion with God. Reconciliation is essential in God's kingdom.

The image is Paul paints in Corinthians is the complete opposite of the individualism that so easily creeps into our churches today. Paul isn't calling us to go it alone, he's inviting us to lean on each other, to build a kind of community where fear, insecurity, and unforgiveness don't get to take root. When we actually live connected, those things lose their power.

Building authentic connections isn't always easy. Let's face it, fear, the constant rush of life, and the pull of "do it yourself" culture can keep us from experiencing the kind of deep relationships we're made for. But here's the good news: we don't have to stay stuck in shallow connections. A simple yet profound starting point is vulnerability and grace.

Vulnerability is often the starting point for real connection. It means being willing to show up without pretending and letting people see the full picture, not just the highlights. That includes the struggles, the doubts, and the parts we usually try to keep hidden. When we open that door and let others in, something sacred begins to happen. We stop performing and start building the kind of relationships where trust and love can take root.

But vulnerability can't thrive without grace. Grace gives relationships the space to breathe. Without it, one mistake or misunderstanding can create distance that's hard to close. The truth is, we're all going to mess up. That's why grace matters so much. It says, "You don't have to be perfect for me to walk with you." Grace makes room for growth. It is what allows people to stay, heal, and become who God has called them to be, even in the middle of their process.

When we start practicing vulnerability and grace, something amazing happens. The walls we've built come down. Trust grows. And people begin to feel safe enough to step into deeper, life-giving connections. Breaking down the barriers to real relationships isn't about trying to fix people or force everything to be perfect. It's about making space, space for God's love to do what only He can do: heal, restore, and transform. Because at the core of it all, that's what the gospel is about. Reconciliation is the key to true unity.

So here's the challenge: What step can you take toward vulnerability this week? Where can you extend grace? Imagine the kind of community we could create if we all started living this way, a place where people feel truly seen, accepted, and loved. That's the kind of connection God designed us for, and it's worth every effort to build.

For believers, authentic connection isn't optional. It's the way we reflect God's love to others and show the world the transformative power of the gospel. When the church lives out reconciliation and interdependence, it becomes a living testimony of God's grace—a place where the disconnected find belonging.

# The Role of Listening in Building Bridges

True listening is one of the most powerful ways to connect with others. It's more than hearing words, it's fully engaging with another person's heart and story. When we truly listen, we create space for people to feel understood. In the church, where relationships can struggle from miscommunication or surface-level engagement, the act of listening becomes an essential bridge.

Listening requires focus and intentionality. Adam S. McHugh, in *The Listening Life*, describes it as a spiritual discipline, noting that real listening can't happen when our attention is divided. This means setting aside distractions and prioritizing someone else's voice over our thoughts or responses. True listening means going beyond the words themselves to understand the emotions, fears, and hopes being shared beneath them.

> *In a world filled with noise, truly hearing someone is a rare and transformative gift.*

When a church learns how to truly listen, it creates space for healing and trust to grow. Leaders who take the time to really hear people, whether it's in a counseling moment or just a casual conversation, set the tone for a culture of empathy and care. It doesn't take much. Just slowing down, asking genuine questions, or giving someone your full attention can go a long way. Those small, intentional choices let people know they matter—and that kind of connection is what builds a community rooted in love and respect.

The beauty of listening is that it's both relational and spiritual. When we listen well, we reflect the heart of Christ, who always made time for the needs of others. In a world filled with noise, truly hearing someone is a rare and transformative gift. By making room for this kind of connection, we create a church culture where every person feels valued, understood, and embraced.

## The Power of Active Listening

Active listening goes beyond hearing words. It requires understanding the heart behind them. It requires empathy, patience, and the willingness to set aside your thoughts or agenda. Truly listening to someone is a rare and powerful way to communicate care and respect. It's an act of humility and love, where you choose to focus fully on the person in front of you, showing them that their voice matters.

In the church, active listening has the power to transform relationships. When leaders listen intentionally, they create an environment of trust where people feel safe sharing their struggles and joys. For members, listening breaks down barriers like misunderstanding and mistrust, fostering unity and deeper connections. It shifts conversations from casual pleasantries to meaningful interactions that reflect the love of Christ and strengthen the bonds within the church community.

The story of Job provides a profound example of the power of listening. After Job's unimaginable loss, his friends came to sit with him in silence for seven days, simply being present in his grief. It wasn't until they began to speak and try to explain his suffering that their presence became more of a burden than a comfort. This story reminds us that sometimes, the best way to support someone is to listen without trying to fix or analyze. True listening creates space for healing and connection, even in the most painful moments.

One of the overlooked benefits of listening is its ability to de-escalate tension. When someone feels heard, their defenses naturally lower, paving the way for better understanding and reconciliation. This makes listening a powerful tool for building relationships and also for resolving conflicts and bridging divides. When everyone's talking, listening becomes a rare and healing gift.

When we prioritize listening, we reflect the love of Christ in a tangible way. Slowing down, asking thoughtful questions, and being fully present shows others, they are valued. It shows them that they matter. It might seem small and simple, but it is more powerful than we think. That kind of intentional care builds stronger relationships and creates trust.

## The Art of Listening Well

Active listening takes practice, but it's one of the most powerful ways to strengthen relationships. It creates a space where people feel safe, understood, and genuinely cared for. This kind of listening takes intentionality, empathy, and a choice to be fully present with the person right in front of you.

Being present is what good listening is built on. Let's be honest, distractions are everywhere. From buzzing phones to running through mental to-do lists, it's easy to be halfway checked out. But when you give someone your full attention, you're saying something powerful: "You matter." That might look like putting your phone on silent, making eye contact, or just being still and truly engaged. These small choices go a long way in building trust and showing real care.

Listening goes beyond simply hearing words. It involves a genuine desire to understand. Asking thoughtful questions like, "Can you tell me more about that?" or reflecting on what you hear can help clarify emotions and intentions. For example, saying, "It sounds like you're feeling overwhelmed because of…" shows that you're not only paying attention but also working to understand their perspective. This approach is especially helpful in resolving conflicts or navigating sensitive conversations.

It's natural to want to fix things when someone shares their struggles, but often, the most loving response is simply to listen. People don't always need advice—they need to feel supported. Offering a validating comment like, "I'm so sorry you're going through this," can be far more comforting than jumping to solutions. When people feel heard, it opens the door for healing and connection, making space for deeper relationships to grow.

By being fully present, seeking understanding, and resisting the urge to fix, we reflect God's love in our interactions. Listening is a skill. It's a gift we give to others, a way to create safe, meaningful connections that transform our church community into a place where everyone feels valued and known.

Listening is an act of worship, a way of honoring the image of God in others. When we take time to hear someone's heart, we're choosing love over hurry, presence over performance. And in doing so, we become a living reflection of Christ's heart in our community.

## Grace in Conflict Resolution

Conflict is inevitable in any relationship, even within the church. Misunderstandings, differing perspectives, and unmet expectations are bound to arise when people share life. But the real issue isn't the presence of conflict—it's how we choose to handle it.

Patrick Lencioni, in *The Five Dysfunctions of a Team,* explains that avoiding conflict often creates deeper divisions over time, while engaging with it in a healthy way builds trust and understanding. The same principle applies to the church. When we avoid addressing tensions, they don't disappear, they quietly grow, straining relationships and unity. But when we approach conflict with humility and grace, it becomes an opportunity for growth, healing, and stronger connections.

Resolving conflict begins with a willingness to listen and seek understanding. Conflict isn't a battleground for pride. It's an opportunity to rebuild what was broken. Jesus offers clear wisdom on addressing conflict in Matthew 18, emphasizing private, respectful conversations as the starting point for reconciliation.

Whether it's a one-on-one discussion or bringing in others to mediate, the focus should always remain on restoring the connection. This doesn't mean avoiding difficult truths but delivering them with love and care, fostering mutual respect.

When we bring God into the process, everything shifts. Inviting God into the process not only paves the way for reconciliation but also strengthens the spiritual bond between those involved. Conflict, though challenging, is an opportunity to reflect Christ's love in action. When we handle conflict with humility, prioritize restoration, and invite God into the conversation, we turn what could divide us into a chance to grow closer together.

## The Heart of Resolving Conflict

Resolving conflict starts with humility. When we're willing to acknowledge our faults and approach conversations with a desire to understand rather than defend, it sets the tone for meaningful dialogue. A church elder once reflected on a disagreement over a ministry decision: "I came into the meeting ready to prove my point," he said, "but when I started by admitting my own missteps, the entire tone shifted." Instead of deepening the divide, the conversation turned into a shared effort to find a solution.

Humility has the power to disarm defensiveness and open the door for an authentic bond.

Reconciliation, not winning, should always be the goal of conflict resolution. This means prioritizing the relationship over the argument and listening with the intent to understand rather than preparing your next response. In Matthew 18:15-17, Jesus offers practical wisdom for addressing conflict, focusing on restoring relationships at every step.

Whether it's a private conversation or a mediated discussion, the emphasis is on healing, not proving who's right. Restoration often requires letting go of the need to have the last word and instead choosing to value the connection over being correct.

Prayer is one of the most powerful tools in resolving conflict. It softens hearts, shifts perspectives, and reminds us of God's presence in the process.

I personally remember how prayer changed the dynamic of a particularly heated disagreement within the leadership team. We paused to pray—not just a quick prayer, but a genuine plea for unity. By the end, there was such a spirit of understanding that we moved forward stronger than before.

Prayer has a way of fostering humility and realigning our focus on Christ, creating space for reconciliation and renewed connection.

Conflict, while challenging, is an opportunity to grow in grace and deepen relationships. When we approach it with humility, prioritize restoration, and invite God into the process, we reflect His love and build a stronger, more united community.

## Rediscovering the Power of Community

Life can feel overwhelming when it seems like everything rests on your shoulders. The constant pressure to manage work, family, and faith alone can leave us feeling stretched thin and disconnected. But the beauty of God's design is that we were never meant to carry life's burdens by ourselves. From the very beginning, He intended for us to live in a community, leaning on one another for support and strength.

If you've ever felt unseen or like you don't matter, let this truth sink in: you play a vital role in what God is building. Your presence, your gifts, your story, they're not small or insignificant. You were created with purpose, and you're an essential part of something much bigger than yourself.

True community isn't about finding flawless people or a perfect church. It's about embracing the imperfections and committing to grow together. The church isn't a showcase of people who have it all figured out. The church is a place where grace is lived out daily. Everyone, from the leader to the newcomer, is in need of support and healing, and it's in that shared vulnerability that genuine relationships flourish.

When it comes to building significant relationships, let's be real, it's not always easy. Fear, busyness, and the pull toward individualism can make connection feel like an uphill battle. But here's the thing: we were never meant to do life alone. Romans 12:10 gives us such a beautiful blueprint for how to move past those barriers: *"Be devoted to one another in love. Honor one another above yourselves."*

What would it look like if we actually lived that out? Being devoted to one another means showing up, even when it's inconvenient. It means prioritizing relationships over our schedules and choosing to see the people in our lives not as interruptions but as gifts.

It's about how we view the people who cross our paths each day, especially when it feels like they're getting in the way of our plans, tasks, or comfort. This challenges us to reframe those moments. Instead of thinking, *"I don't have time for this,"* we pause and think, *"Maybe this person is a gift from God—a chance to love, to be present, or to grow."* I like to call these moments, divine interruptions.

Jesus did this all the time. He constantly allowed Himself to be "interrupted", by the bleeding woman, the blind man calling out, the children the disciples tried to shoo away. And yet, He treated each one like they mattered deeply.

Relationships thrive when we put love into action. They grow through presence and not the pressure to be perfect. When we let go of the need to impress or perform and instead focus on loving and honoring each other, something shifts. Walls come down. Trust is built. And the messy, beautiful work of community begins.

Romans 12:10 is a call to live differently. It's a reminder that the way we love and honor one another has the power to transform not only our relationships but also the world around us. So, let's start there, with a love that's devoted, intentional, and willing to go beyond the surface.

If you've ever doubted your place in the church, remember that God designed you to be part of His family. Belonging isn't about fitting into someone else's expectations; it's about stepping into the unique role God has for you in His body. Together, we can rediscover the joy and strength that comes from living in a real, authentic community.

## Cultivating a Relational Ministry

Creating a culture of authentic connection in the church doesn't happen by chance. It requires intentionality and effort. It's not this hyper focus on Sunday services or well-organized events; but about doing life together. Real relationships are often built in small, ordinary moments, like conversations over a meal or spontaneous acts of kindness. These are the spaces where connections deepen.

Leadership plays a crucial role in setting the tone for relational ministry. When leaders are honest about their challenges and victories, they create an environment where others feel safe to do the same. Vulnerability from leaders signals that authenticity is valued, encouraging everyone to bring their whole selves into the community. It's not about leaders bearing every burden in public but about modeling a culture where no one feels the need to hide behind perfection.

Celebrating moments of unity is another essential practice. Whether it's a small group rallying around a member in need or a congregation working together on a service project, these shared experiences reinforce the beauty of connection. Highlighting these moments helps the church see the value of collaboration and builds a sense of collective purpose.

> *The church thrives when we intentionally foster a culture of connection.*

At its heart, cultivating a relational ministry is about creating a church that feels like family, a place where people are truly known, embraced as they are, and invited to grow together in love and purpose.

It's about living out the love of Christ, ensuring that every interaction reflects His grace and care.

This kind of culture isn't built overnight, but it's worth the effort. When relationships are prioritized over programs, and connection over convenience, the church becomes a living example of His love. Together, we can build a community where authenticity thrives, grace abounds, and no one walks alone.

## Rooted in Relationships

Authentic connection is a mirror of God's heart, not just a milestone we hope to reach. When we face relational barriers, resolve conflicts with grace, and embrace our shared identity in Christ, we create a church that goes beyond the gatherings.

Healthy relationships don't happen by accident, they take intentional effort and a willingness to grow together. That's where the gospel comes alive: in the daily choices and the tough conversations. The church thrives when we foster a culture of connection, one that reflects the love and unity that Christ modeled.

When we settle for surface-level interactions, the church becomes more of a crowd than a community. Instead of reflecting God's love, we risk misrepresenting it, turning faith into a message we preach but don't live. Without real connection, people slip through the cracks, and the transformative power of love is reduced to words with no weight.

But when we decide to choose to connect deeply, we show the world a picture of God's transformative love. This is a rhythm we're called to live out every day. Together, we can build a community where God's love is more than a message; it's an experience shared in every relationship and every moment.

# Chapter 6
# Transformation Through Relationship

Something isn't quite right.

We see it, we hear it, and if we're honest, we feel it, too.

For years, discipleship in many churches has been shaped by programs. There's a formula for everything: Bible studies on Monday, small groups on Wednesday, and leadership classes sprinkled throughout the year. On paper, it all seems solid, structured, organized, and consistent. And to be clear, there's nothing wrong with any of that. But if you pause and ask believers what discipleship actually means to them, their answers might surprise you. Or worse, they might not have an answer at all.

Here's the truth: you can't talk about building a relational church without talking about building people. Programs can provide structure, but they can't replace personal transformation. Discipleship and spiritual formation are the soil where relational depth takes root.

Is Spiritual Formation the Same as Discipleship?

A lot of people use the words discipleship and spiritual formation as if they're interchangeable, but they're not quite the same. They're connected, like two sides of the same coin, but they serve different purposes in our journey with Jesus. And understanding the difference? That's a game-changer.

## Discipleship: The Journey of Following Jesus

Discipleship is all about learning to follow Jesus. It's an intentional decision to walk with Him, learn from Him, and let His teachings shape every area of our lives. The word disciple literally means learner—so at its core, discipleship is about being a student of Jesus, not only in theory, but in how we live, love, and lead.

Think about how Jesus discipled His followers. Jesus didn't stop at teaching truths. He called people to follow a new way of living. He said, "Follow me, and I will make you fishers of men" (Matthew 4:19). He walked with them, ate with them, laughed with them, and even challenged them when they got it wrong. It was personal. It was relational. It wasn't about checking off a set of religious tasks; it was about growing into the kind of people who would reflect Him in the world.

Different theological traditions describe discipleship in unique ways:

- Wesleyan Perspective – John Wesley saw discipleship as a lifelong pursuit of holiness. It wasn't simply believing the right things; it was about growing in grace, practicing spiritual disciplines, and being shaped by a deep, intentional community. Wesley's famous class meetings were spaces where people could be real about their struggles and help each other grow.

- Reformed Perspective – In the Reformed tradition, discipleship is seen as God's sovereign work in shaping believers. What we do matters, but even more important is how God transforms us through His Word and Spirit. As Philippians 2:13 says, "For it is God who works in you to will and to act in order to fulfill His good purpose."
- Catholic Perspective – Catholic theology views discipleship as spiritual apprenticeship, a lifelong process of learning from Jesus through Scripture, sacraments, and active faith. It's about being formed in Christ through the life of the Church.

No matter the tradition, one thing is clear: discipleship is active. It's a journey that requires movement, obedience, and a willingness to be shaped by Jesus.

## Spiritual Formation: The Deep Inner Work of Becoming Like Christ

While discipleship is about following, spiritual formation is about being formed. It's the deep, often unseen work that happens in our hearts as we grow into the image of Christ. The goal isn't to add more to your schedule. It's to become more patient, more loving, and more in tune with the heart of God.

- Dallas Willard describes spiritual formation as "the process by which the human spirit or will is given a definite form or character." In other words, gaining knowledge is only part of the journey. The deeper work happens when we allow God to reshape who we are at the core *(Renovation of the Heart)*.

- Wesleyan Perspective – In Wesleyan theology, spiritual formation is tied to sanctification, the process of becoming more like Jesus. Wesley called this Christian perfection, not in the sense of being flawless, but in having a heart completely surrendered to God.

- Reformed Perspective – In Reformed thought, spiritual formation is the work of the Holy Spirit, shaping us through Scripture, prayer, and community. Romans 12:2 captures it well: "Do not conform to the pattern of this world but be transformed by the renewing of your mind."

Unlike discipleship, which involves external movement (learning, following, teaching), spiritual formation is the internal shaping that happens along the way. It's the deep, slow work of God changing our desires, our perspectives, and our hearts. You can be part of a discipleship group and still not experience real spiritual formation if your heart isn't being changed. Likewise, you can be spiritually formed over time without being in a formal discipleship program.

## The Key Difference: Movement vs. Transformation

If discipleship is the journey, spiritual formation is the shaping that happens on the journey. Discipleship is about action, while spiritual formation is about becoming. One is about learning to follow Jesus; the other is about being transformed by Him.

The two are deeply connected. Healthy discipleship should always lead to spiritual formation, and real spiritual formation should make us even more committed disciples. But when discipleship becomes just a program or a checklist, it can feel hollow. And when spiritual formation is seen as just a personal, internal process, it can become detached from real-world faith. We need both.

Jesus taught His disciples and formed them. And that's what He calls us into today. Not only to follow, but to be transformed. Not just to learn, but to become. When we get this right, it changes everything about how we grow in our faith, how we lead others, and how we build communities where real transformation happens.

## When Discipleship Feels Hollow

Here's the tension: how is it that in a world full of resources, content, and church programs, so many people feel spiritually disconnected, disillusioned, and unheard?

We've confused activity with impact.
We've confused programs with progress.
And we've confused information with transformation.

Discipleship was never meant to be about checking boxes or following a pre-planned curriculum, it's about movement, growth, and direction. Discipleship is not about perfection but direction toward Christ. It's about learning while becoming, and that shift in perspective changes everything.

## The Struggle with Impersonal Discipleship

Believers today are wrestling with real-life questions:

- How do I navigate relationships without losing myself?
- How do I live out my faith when it feels like no one around me is doing the same?
- Does the church actually care about me, or am I just another seat in the room?

Many of our current models often only offer rehearsed answers instead of walking the journey with people. Too often, discipleship feels like a script, polished, predictable, and disconnected from real life. We have answers ready before the questions are even asked.

We share principles when people need presence. We offer solutions to struggles we haven't stopped to understand. In this model, discipleship becomes less about meeting people where they are and more about moving them through a curriculum, step-by-step, as if spiritual growth is something you can manufacture on a timeline.

Spiritual formation happens in community, not in isolation. A disciple cannot grow in a vacuum. We need people who challenge us, encourage us, and walk with us through both victories and struggles. Without genuine relationships, discipleship becomes a hollow exercise, full of lessons but lacking in life.

In our current model, discipleship has become a classroom rather than a life shared. We gather people into rooms, hand them notebooks, and teach them *about* God, but we rarely teach them how to experience Him. We mistake attendance for transformation and participation for growth. The classroom is clean and controlled, there's little room for doubt, struggle, or imperfection.

True discipleship doesn't happen when people are sitting in rows, staring at whiteboards. It happens over dinner tables, in late-night phone calls, and through conversations where people feel heard and understood. Instead of handing someone a lesson plan, discipleship calls us to walk with them through the real rhythms of life.

When discipleship becomes impersonal, it stops being effective. People want to hear truths; but they want to see those truths lived out in others. They want to experience the love of God in relationships that are consistent, honest, and intentional. And because of that, they start to believe the church—and maybe even God—has nothing to say about the realities they face. But it doesn't have to stay that way. The beautiful thing about discipleship is that we already have the model we need. Jesus showed us what it looks like to invest in people's lives in a way that transforms them.

Discipleship was never meant to be a program; it was always meant to be personal. When we look at Jesus' life, we see a different way. Jesus didn't teach from a distance or sit in a temple and wait for people to come to Him.

> *People want to hear truths; but hey want to see those truths lived out in others.*

He went to where people were. He walked dusty roads with His disciples, shared meals with them, laughed with them, and wept with them. Yes, He taught them what to believe; but He also showed them how to live.

The Church exists today because Jesus went beyond preaching to the crowds. He invested deeply in twelve young men, walking with them, loving them, correcting them, and shaping them. That's the power of personal discipleship.

Think about that for a moment. Jesus, the Son of God, chose to spend three years pouring into twelve ordinary people. He knew their struggles. He called out their doubts. He challenged them to grow. And He did it all in the context of relationship. He shared life with them in a way that was real, raw, and consistent.

His model was relational, not transactional. Transformational, not superficial. There's a reason the disciples were willing to lay down their lives for the gospel. It wasn't because Jesus gave them a great program to follow. It was because He gave them Himself. The transformation they experienced wasn't the result of a system or a curriculum, it was the result of a relationship.

The same is true for us today. Discipleship can't simply be about a set of principles or a series of steps. It's not something you can manufacture or measure with checkboxes. It's personal. It's relational. And when it's done right, it's life changing.

Discipleship and spiritual formation are not reserved for church leaders. They are a calling for every believer. However, leaders play a unique role in creating the kind of culture where growth happens. When leaders model what it means to follow Jesus, not just teaching but living it out, they set the tone for others. It's not about perfection; it's about authenticity and a willingness to invest in people. Leaders who prioritize relationships over programs and heart transformation over performance inspire others to do the same.

For church members, discipleship isn't something to "leave to the leaders." Everyone has a role to play. Whether it's mentoring someone, encouraging a friend, or simply living in a way that points people to Jesus, discipleship is something we all share. The church thrives when both leaders and members commit to walking this journey together.

Leaders create the space, but it's the everyday connections, conversations, accountability, and showing up for one another, that make spiritual formation real. When leaders and members embrace discipleship together, the impact goes beyond individual growth. It transforms the entire church into a place where people truly grow and lives are deeply impacted.

Discipleship and spiritual formation are vital for both leaders and church members because they shape the culture of the church as a whole. Leaders set the tone by modeling a life of authentic growth and prioritizing relationships over programs.

When both leaders and members embrace this journey together, the church becomes a place of transformation, where people grow, relationships deepen, and lives are impacted for generations.

## Shaping the Heart, Not Just the Mind

The issue we are facing is that transactional faith leaves us empty. Have you ever felt like you're just going through the motions in your walk with God? Maybe you're attending church, reading your Bible, or even joining a small group, but something still feels off. That's what happens when discipleship becomes more about information than transformation. It emphasizes learning about God without actually drawing near to Him or experiencing real connection.

The problem is, when we make discipleship all about knowledge or tasks, we miss the heart of it: *relationship*. Growing in Christ means more than filling our minds with facts; it's about letting those truths transform who we are and how we live. It's easy to know a lot about God without actually knowing Him.

Relational depth—the kind of connection that changes us from the inside out—is the key. Without it, our faith can feel shallow, even empty.

At its core, spiritual formation is the journey of allowing God to transform who you are from the inside out. As Dallas Willard puts it, *"The most important thing in your life is not what you do; it's who you become."* In other words, God's greatest desire is not for you to simply do things for Him but to become someone who reflects Him in every part of your life.

Think about it, Jesus didn't call His disciples to follow Him so they could just gain more knowledge. He called them to walk with Him, to learn His ways, and to have their hearts transformed in the process. Being transformed to reflect Christ's character, His love, humility, patience, and kindness, is the ultimate goal of discipleship. It's about becoming a person whose life naturally bears the fruit of the Spirit (Galatians 5:22-23) because they're deeply rooted in their relationship with God.

But this kind of transformation doesn't happen through an exchange-based faith—where we simply check off spiritual to-dos like Bible reading plans, church attendance, or volunteer hours. It happens when we lean into a relational faith. This means making space for intimacy with God, being vulnerable with Him, and letting His Spirit work in the messy, hidden parts of our hearts. Transformation is not something we can manufacture; it's something God produces in us as we abide in Him (John 15:5).

> Transformation is not something we can manufacture; it's something God produces in us as we abide in Him

Moving from transactional to relational faith changes everything. Instead of asking, *"What can I do for God?"* we start asking, *"How is God shaping me to be more like Him?"* This shift takes away the pressure to perform and lets us rest in the truth that God cares more about our closeness to Him than our productivity. As we draw closer to Him, He reshapes our priorities, our relationships, and, ultimately, our lives.

## The Danger of 'Doing' Over 'Being'

Let's talk about something that trips a lot of us up: the pressure to always *do*. In church culture, it's easy to think that our spiritual health is tied to how busy we are. We measure growth by how many ministries we're part of, how much we volunteer, or how often we show up. But here's the problem, when we focus too much on *doing*, we forget about *being*.

Author Henri Nouwen captures this perfectly when he says, *"Being busy has become a sign of importance, but it has little to do with true discipleship."* In other words, God isn't impressed by our schedules. What He cares about is our hearts.

When we focus on *doing*, we risk burnout. We might look like we've got it all together on the outside, but inside, we're drained. True spiritual growth comes from being with Jesus, abiding in Him like the branches abide in the vine (John 15:5). From that place of connection, our actions flow naturally, rooted in love rather than obligation.

Think about it: when Martha was busy serving in Luke 10:38-42, Jesus didn't rebuke her for working, He reminded her that Mary, who sat at His feet, had chosen what was *better*. Sometimes, we need to slow down and focus on being in God's presence before we rush into doing things for Him.

No matter where you are in your faith journey, the starting point is the same: it begins with connecting with Jesus. For those who don't see themselves as leaders, this means focusing on the basics. Spend time with Him, not out of obligation, but to deepen your relationship. Pray, journal, or simply sit quietly and let His Spirit speak to your heart.

For leaders, the challenge often looks different. It's easy to fall into the trap of tying your value to what you accomplish, the number of people you disciple, the programs you lead, or the tasks you complete. But discipleship isn't a task; it's a relational investment.

True leadership in the faith means walking alongside others, sharing life with them, and showing them how to follow Jesus by your example. Teaching matters, but what shapes hearts for Christ is the way we care and how deeply we walk with others.

Discipleship was never meant to be a set of steps to complete. It's so much more than programs or classes, it's a shared journey, a life-on-life investment that helps us grow into the image of Christ. Francis Chan, in *Letters to the Church*, hits the nail on the head when he says, "We've made discipleship a series of classes when it was always meant to be a relationship." And isn't that the truth? We've overcomplicated something Jesus modeled so simply and beautifully.

This is an invitation to rethink discipleship , not as a checklist or a set of rules, but as something personal and messy. True discipleship grows through honest relationships and shared journeys with Christ at the center. Checklists and class attendance won't get you there.

It's about walking alongside someone, sharing the highs and lows, and growing together in faith. This kind of relational discipleship is where real transformation happens, through accountability, vulnerability, and those raw, honest moments that just can't be manufactured in a classroom.

When we embrace this approach, discipleship stops feeling like another task and instead it becomes a way of life. It's showing up, staying present, and trusting God to do the work through our relationships. As we invest in others, God uses those connections to spark growth, healing, and transformation, in their lives and in ours. The ripple effects of that kind of love and investment go further than we can imagine.

So here's the challenge: Who can you walk alongside right now? Who can you invest in, not only with your words, but with your time and presence? Relational discipleship isn't about being perfect or having all the answers. It's about being available, being real, and letting God use you to shape lives for His glory. This is the heart of discipleship, one relationship at a time.

This idea challenges the notion that discipleship is merely about structured programs or intellectual growth. Bonhoeffer believed that transformation happens when believers walk together, carrying each other's burdens and encouraging one another in the faith. It's in this shared life—praying together, struggling together, and celebrating together—that hearts are truly changed. His reflections remind us that discipleship is relational at its core and that the greatest impact often comes through authentic, life-on-life connections.

This is the heart of discipleship: moving past an information-based faith and stepping into a relationship with Jesus that transforms us from the inside out. It's not about doing more; it's about becoming more like Him.

## Why We Grow Together

Today, isolation has become the norm for so many people, even in the church. It's easy to slip in and out of a Sunday service without connecting with anyone or to keep our struggles hidden because we're afraid of judgment or rejection. For some, faith has become a private matter, something to be managed on their own rather than shared. But here's the problem: we weren't designed to grow in isolation.

The Bible is clear—faith flourishes in community. When we try to do it alone, we miss out on the encouragement, accountability, and challenge that comes from walking alongside others. Discipleship that happens in isolation often leads to stagnation. We might look fine on the outside, but inwardly, we struggle to grow, heal, and thrive in our faith.

## True Growth Happens Together

Proverbs 27:17 puts it beautifully: *"As iron sharpens iron, so one person sharpens another."* We need each other to grow, to learn, and to become the people God has called us to be. When believers encourage, challenge, and support one another, faith deepens and matures in ways it simply can't when we're alone.

True engagement goes beyond simply attending church or joining a group. It calls us to connect deeply with one another. Growth doesn't happen in idealized, picture-perfect settings; it happens in the messy, real-world moments where we learn to love, forgive, and walk with each other through the highs and lows of life.

It's difficult to mature in faith alone. God designed us to grow through relationships. Hebrews 10:24-25 reminds us, *"And let us consider how we may spur one another on toward love and good deeds, not giving up meeting together, as some are in the habit of doing, but encouraging one another, and all the more as you see the Day approaching."* Community is essential to living out the gospel.

But here's the challenge: are we actually engaging in an authentic community, or are we just sharing space?

I've been part of churches where people faithfully attend and serve week after week, but they don't really know anything about each other. It felt more like being co-workers than family—like showing up to do a job rather than sharing life together.

One church I was part of reminded me of going to a theme park. You're surrounded by people, maybe even doing the same things, but there's no genuine bond. Everyone's busy moving from one attraction to the next, and at the end of the day, you go home without ever truly engaging with the people you were around.

That's not the kind of community God calls us to. The church is more than a place for serving side by side. It's a space where we truly know one another, encourage one another, and grow together.

If we settle for shallow connections, we miss out on the depth and richness of relationships that God uses to shape us into His image. Biblical togetherness requires vulnerability, intentionality, and a willingness to go beyond surface-level interactions. And it's in that kind of community that faith truly grows and thrives.

## A Safe Space for Growth

Accountability and intentional relationships are at the heart of spiritual formation. Growth happens when we allow others to speak into our lives, to challenge us when we're off track, encourage us when we're struggling, and celebrate with us in moments of victory. But accountability isn't about control or judgment. It's about creating a safe, loving environment where someone can ask, "How's your walk with God?" This kind of relationship goes beyond surface-level connections and dives into the deeper issues of the heart, fostering growth that isolation can never achieve.

Relational discipleship also leaves a legacy of faith. It's about the here and now; but also about impacting generations. When we invest in others through intentional, Christ-centered relationships, it extends far beyond us. Paul's relationship with Timothy is a beautiful example of this. He poured into him as a spiritual father, equipping him to carry on the work of the gospel. That kind of relational investment builds a faith foundation that can withstand the test of time.

> *Growth happens when we allow others to speak into our lives*

True community creates a space where people feel safe to grow. It's in these environments, where grace meets truth, that we can ask hard questions, wrestle with struggles, and live out the gospel together. Growth doesn't require perfection; it requires a willingness to be vulnerable. When the church becomes a place where authenticity is valued, and relationships are prioritized, people can experience the kind of transformation that only happens through sincere relationships.

Whether you see yourself as a leader or not, the truth is, we all need community. Maybe for you, that looks like jumping into a small group, finding a mentor, or having someone you trust who can check in on your walk with God. It doesn't have to be anything formal or complicated, it just has to be real. It's about showing up for each other and letting others show up for you too.

If you're a leader, the real challenge is creating space where relational discipleship can actually grow. That goes way beyond planning Bible studies or running programs. It's about building an environment where people feel safe to be real, ask questions, and grow at their own pace. As a leader, you set the tone by being honest, showing vulnerability, and choosing people over performance.

Discipleship goes beyond sharing information. It's about walking through life with someone, nurturing their growth, and equipping them to do the same for others. It's not just a leader's job either. This kind of relational investment is something every believer is called to, and it's how real transformation happens.

## The Power of Walking Together

Paul and Timothy's relationship is one of the most powerful examples of discipleship in the Bible. Paul, a seasoned apostle, met Timothy, a young believer with great potential, during his missionary journeys.

Seeing something special in Timothy, Paul took him under his wing, not simply to teach him about faith but to mentor him on how to live it out. Over time, their relationship grew into something much deeper. Paul referred to Timothy as his *"true son in the faith"* (1 Timothy 1:2), showing how personal and invested their bond became.

Paul shared his life with him. He encouraged Timothy when he felt timid, gave him guidance on leading others, and passed down wisdom that would help him grow spiritually and practically.

In *2 Timothy 2:2*, Paul charged Timothy to take what he had learned and pass it on to others: *"The things you have heard me say in the presence of many witnesses entrust to reliable people who will also be qualified to teach others."* This wasn't just a one-time mentorship; it was the beginning of a spiritual inheritance, a ripple effect that would continue through generations.

From Timothy's perspective, this relationship went beyond receiving guidance; it was transformational. Timothy grew in confidence and faith because he had someone who believed in him, poured into him, and modeled what it meant to follow Jesus. Paul's investment in Timothy went beyond leadership development. He focused on shaping Timothy's identity in Christ and guiding him to live out his faith with authenticity.

Timothy shows us what's possible when someone leans into relational discipleship. He didn't start out as a leader, he was just a young guy who was hungry to grow. His story reminds us that being discipled isn't about having it all together or holding a title. It's about being open, teachable, and willing to let someone walk with you, speak into your life, and help you grow in your faith.

Whether you're mentoring like Paul or learning like Timothy, this kind of connection has the power to change lives and strengthen the entire church. Faith was never meant to be a solo journey. We grow the most when we're surrounded by real relationships, people who hold us up, call us out, and walk with us through all of life's highs and lows.

You might be just stepping into community for the first time, or you could be leading others in their faith journey. No matter where you are, discipleship is all about doing life together. It's about encouraging one another, challenging each other to grow, and building a faith that doesn't stop with us, it carries into the next generation. Leaning into real community creates a space for shared growth, where we don't walk alone but grow side by side, like a family.

## The Heart of Relational Discipleship

Spiritual growth is about forming habits that align our hearts with God's character—habits that transform what we do and who we are becoming. Habits shape our lives in powerful ways, and when they're rooted in relational discipleship, they outlast programs and structures.

The contrast between being part of a class and walking closely with someone who speaks into your life is significant. A discipleship class might teach you biblical principles but walking with someone brings those principles to life. It's the difference between hearing about love and living it out.

As author James K.A. Smith writes in *You Are What You Love*, "Our hearts are shaped by what we worship and what we repeatedly do." Programs can inform us, but relationships transform us by modeling Christ-like habits that stick.

Relational discipleship creates space for habits to take root in ways that programs alone can't. It's the shared life that makes discipleship personal. When someone invites you into their world, showing you how to pray, how to study Scripture, and how to live out faith in the daily grind, those habits become part of you. They're no longer something you do, they're part of who you are.

Walking closely with someone also keeps us anchored when life gets hard. Unlike a program, a relationship provides accountability, encouragement, and real-time wisdom. Dietrich Bonhoeffer, in *Life Together*, emphasized this when he said, *"The Christian needs another Christian who speaks God's Word to him. He needs him again and again when he becomes uncertain and discouraged."* Relationships keep our spiritual habits alive, even when the motivation to keep going fades.

At the heart of it all is Scripture. God's Word is the foundation for habits that truly transform. Without it, discipleship becomes aimless, floating on personal opinions instead of divine truth. As Paul reminds us in *2 Timothy 3:16*, *"All Scripture is God-breathed and is useful for teaching, rebuking, correcting and training in righteousness."* Scripture keeps everything grounded. It anchors habits, fuels growth, and aligns us with God's character.

## A Shared Journey of Growth and Legacy

Discipleship and spiritual formation are about a shared journey. This journey isn't something we take alone; it shapes our character, deepens our faith, and connects us to one another. At its heart, discipleship is about transformation, letting God work in us so that we reflect Christ in every area of our lives.

Transformation over information is the key. Knowledge by itself doesn't lead to real change, but when we allow God to shape our hearts, something shifts. Growth happens when we move beyond just learning and start becoming. Who we're becoming matters more than what we've accomplished. That truth pushes us to embrace habits and rhythms that form us into the image of Christ, day by day.

Accountability and relational investment are the lifeblood of discipleship. Investing in relationships is what makes discipleship real. When we walk alongside others, we sharpen one another, as Proverbs 27:17 says: *"As iron sharpens iron, so one person sharpens another."* Relational discipleship invites us into a community where we can grow together, holding each other accountable and encouraging one another toward love and good deeds (Hebrews 10:24-25).

Scripture is the unshakable foundation of all spiritual growth. Without it, discipleship loses its direction. God's Word anchors us, equips us, and gives us the wisdom we need for every step of the journey. Leaders and non-leaders alike need Scripture as the guide that keeps discipleship centered on divine truth, not human opinion.

Discipleship takes root when what we learn becomes how we live and when that life becomes an example for those following behind us. When we invest in one person, that investment cascades, touching lives far beyond what we can see or imagine.

No matter where you are in your journey, whether you're leading others or just taking your first steps, the call remains the same:

- Step into discipleship.

- Pursue transformation over mere information.
- Build relationships that keep you accountable, encourage your growth, and point you back to Jesus.
- Root yourself in Scripture, creating a foundation of faith that lasts not just for your lifetime, but for generations to come.

Growth isn't a solo journey. It takes place as we walk alongside others in faith, becoming a stronger family together.

Discipleship and spiritual growth aren't meant to happen in a vacuum. Yes, personal faith matters, but the environment we're in plays a huge role in whether that growth really takes root. That's where culture comes in. When we create spaces filled with trust, accountability, and encouragement, we shape how people grow today and for generations to come.

The legacy of discipleship depends not only on the seeds we plant but on the condition of the soil, hearts prepared to receive, grow, and multiply. And if a church is going to be a place of real transformation, someone has to lead the way. That starts with the leader.

# Chapter 7
# Prioritizing Relational Leadership

The truth is, many church leaders today feel stuck, isolated, burnt out, and unsure of how to bridge the growing gap between themselves and the people they're called to serve. For some, that gap has become so wide that leadership feels more like a burden than the calling it was meant to be.

Then you add in the voices of disillusioned Christians, those who've felt hurt, ignored, or pushed aside, and suddenly, the church can feel like anything but the relational, connected community Christ intended it to be.

If you've ever felt overlooked by the church or like it cared more about programs than people, you're not the only one. Maybe you've had moments where a leader's actions didn't reflect the kind of care or support you needed. Or maybe you've been caught in the middle of church politics that felt more like a battle than a place of belonging. Experiences like that leave a mark. And the truth is, real leadership, leadership that reflects the heart of Jesus, has to start with genuine care for people. Without that, everything else starts to fall apart.

Church leadership comes with real challenges. Beyond the sermon, the vision, and the logistics, it all comes down to caring for people. And let's face it: people can be messy and complicated. But they're also the heart of what the church is all about.

Leading in the church was never meant to be about managing tasks, planning events, or checking off boxes. It's about people, walking with them, investing in their growth, and building the kind of environment where relationships actually have room to grow. Relational leaders make space for others to thrive. And that means being present, even when it's uncomfortable, messy, or inconvenient, because that's where real ministry happens.

For leaders, this is where the challenge and opportunity collide. The church is filled with people carrying wounds, some visible, some hidden. And as leaders, the question isn't whether these wounds exist; it's whether we're willing to step into them.

Can we create spaces where people feel safe?

Because if we want the church to be the relational body of Christ, it starts with showing up in the places where people feel the most unseen. It starts with listening, validating, and rebuilding trust.

You might know what it feels like to experience a disconnect—to wonder if the church really gets the pressures and challenges of life right now. And honestly, that can be a heavy feeling. When the place that's supposed to represent God's love misses the mark, it can leave you questioning where you belong or if you belong at all. Those moments can be painful, but they don't have to define your story. They're worth naming, especially if we want to heal, rebuild trust, and move toward something better.

## The Disconnect Between Leaders and People

One of the biggest challenges church leaders are facing right now is the growing disconnect between the altar and the chairs. Somewhere along the way, something shifted. What started as a call to shepherd hearts began to feel more like managing systems and keeping everything running. And for many people sitting in the congregation, it's starting to feel like there's this quiet distance between them and the ones leading.

That divide wasn't always intentional, sometimes it's just what happens when leaders are carrying so much and don't know where to lay it down. But over time, that distance becomes a wall. And if we're not careful, that wall starts to feel normal, even though deep down, none of us want it there.

But the thing is, this gap isn't something only the congregation feels, leaders feel it too. They're carrying so much behind the scenes, trying to be everything all at once: counselors, teachers, visionaries, conflict-resolvers... and now somehow expected to be social media-savvy on top of it all. And while doing all that, there's this unspoken pressure to look like everything's perfect, to have the flawless marriage, the well-behaved family, and a faith that never wavers.

It's a lot. And for many leaders, trying to hold it all together becomes too heavy. So, they build emotional walls, not because they don't care, but because they don't know how to carry the weight without breaking down.

This emotional distance creates a perfect storm for disillusionment. People in the congregation start to feel like their leaders don't see them, while leaders feel disconnected from the very people they're trying to serve. And before long, we start hearing the same quiet frustration echoed in churches everywhere: *"Something about this just feels… impersonal."*

This impacts both leaders and congregants in profound ways.

For people in the congregation, it often begins as a quiet thought: *"Does anyone here really see me?"* Over time, this feeling grows into frustration or even withdrawal. When leaders seem unreachable or consumed by responsibilities, it's easy for people to feel like they're simply another face in the crowd rather than a valued member of a spiritual family. Leadership is less about power and more about empowering others. When people don't feel empowered, they disengage from the church, and sometimes from their faith altogether.

> **Leadership is less about power and more about empowering others.**

For leaders, the experience isn't all that different. The demands of ministry can feel like an endless list of problems to solve, and the weight of responsibility can be isolating. The connection that once fueled their passion for ministry, the joy of walking with people through life's highs and lows, starts to fade.

Instead of building meaningful relationships, leaders can find themselves caught in a cycle of doing *for* people rather than being *with* them. The result is disconnection from their congregants and from the heart of why they stepped into leadership in the first place.

And then we hear it, the phrase that cuts deep: *"The church feels impersonal."* It's a statement that speaks to a longing for connection, for the church to be what it was always meant to be: a place where people feel known, cared for, and valued.

But when that doesn't happen, it's disappointing and disillusioning. It leaves people questioning not only the church's role in their lives but sometimes even their faith. For leaders, hearing this sentiment can feel like a personal failure, deepening the divide even further.

## Why Relational Leadership Feels Hard

Patrick Lencioni's *The Five Dysfunctions of a Team* sheds light on this dynamic. Lencioni talks about how the lack of trust is the root issue that breaks down healthy teams and you can see that play out in church leadership, too. A lot of leaders feel like they can't be real with the people they serve. And honestly, it's because being vulnerable takes trust. But when you're carrying so much and the pressure feels high, opening up can feel like too big of a risk.

He writes, "Trust is the foundation of real teamwork. And trust is about vulnerability, the willingness to admit mistakes, to ask for help, and to accept feedback." But here's the thing: vulnerability feels risky, especially in the church. Leaders may fear that admitting their struggles will cause people to lose respect for them, while congregants might hesitate to open up because they see their leaders as unapproachable or "too busy."

The lack of vulnerability creates a relational vacuum, leaving both leaders and congregants feeling disconnected. Over time, this can lead to disengagement, with leaders retreating further into their responsibilities and congregants checking out emotionally, spiritually, or even physically. In many church spaces, leadership has become more about control and efficiency than about presence and care.

When there's no room for vulnerability, it leaves a gap in relationships that everyone feels, both leaders and the people they're trying to serve. It's like talking to someone through a thick glass wall. You can see them, but the connection just doesn't land.

For leaders, the pressure to always look strong and put-together can push them to hide behind their responsibilities. It feels safer to stay busy with planning sermons, managing the budget, and running programs than to step into the real, often messy work of building deeper relationships. But without that connection, something important gets lost.

For churchgoers, that lack of vulnerability can be just as damaging. When leaders seem distant or unreachable, it's easy for people to feel like they don't matter, like their struggles are invisible. Church begins to feel less like a family and more like a place you show up to out of habit.

Over time, that disconnection can lead to emotional disengagement. People stop opening up about their real struggles or sharing their joys because they don't feel safe. They might keep attending, but their involvement becomes surface-level, a kind of "sit in the back and leave quietly" approach to church.

For some, that emotional disengagement turns into spiritual disconnection. When the church doesn't feel like a place where they can be real, they start to question if it's worth being there at all. Faith can start to feel like a solo journey instead of something to be shared in the community. And eventually, some may even disengage physically, slipping away from the church altogether. They may not leave with dramatic exits or bold declarations; they simply stop showing up.

The real tragedy is what's lost in the process. People leave behind the potential for life-giving relationships, spiritual growth, and the kind of support that can only come from a connected community. Leaders miss out, too—on the richness of walking closely with the people they're called to serve and the mutual encouragement that comes from shared vulnerability.

But it doesn't have to stay this way. When leaders and congregants commit to fostering authenticity and connection, it can transform the culture of the church. Vulnerability isn't weakness; it's the foundation of trust. And trust is where real relationships—and real ministry—begin.

## The Illusion of Connection

Nowhere is this disconnect more obvious than on social media. Platforms like Instagram, TikTok, and even YouTube have transformed the way church leaders are perceived. On one hand, these platforms offer an incredible opportunity to reach people beyond the four walls of the church. Leaders can share sermons, devotional thoughts, and personal reflections with thousands of people at a time.

But, social media also creates a dangerous illusion of connection. Just because someone "likes" a post doesn't mean they feel truly seen. Just because a leader shares an inspirational quote, or a polished video doesn't mean they're effectively shepherding their people. For many congregants, the curated version of leadership they see online feels distant, unattainable, and, at times, disingenuous.

Younger generations, in particular, are hungry for authenticity. They've grown up in a world of filters and perfectly crafted narratives, and they can spot the difference between surface-level engagement and genuine connection. Leaders who rely too heavily on social media to foster relationships risk missing the point entirely. "Likes" don't replace love, and followers don't replace fellowship.

And that's where the idea of digital discipleship comes in.

There's something really valuable about the heart behind digital discipleship. It's made spiritual content more accessible than ever and created new ways for people to engage with truth. But the downside is, it can easily stop at content consumption.

The risk is that people become *viewers of faith, not participants in it.* They stay hidden behind screens, never having to be honest about their struggles, ask hard questions, or step into real accountability. Digital discipleship has value, but on its own, it can fall short without real, face-to-face community. It can support spiritual growth, but it was never meant to replace the life-on-life connection that forms us into disciples of Jesus.

Younger generations, especially Millennials and Gen Z, have been shaped by a culture saturated with curated perfection. They've spent their lives scrolling through highlight reels on social media, and they've learned to spot inauthenticity from a mile away. What they crave isn't another polished performance or carefully filtered moment. They're looking for leaders who are real, honest, and willing to show their humanity.

Brené Brown, in her book *Daring Greatly*, writes, "Vulnerability is not about winning or losing; it's having the courage to show up when you can't control the outcome." For younger generations, that kind of courage—the willingness to admit mistakes and share struggles—is what makes a leader trustworthy and relatable.

The danger of relying too much on social media to build relationships is that it can give the illusion of connection without the substance. People might double-tap a post or leave a comment, but that doesn't mean they feel genuinely seen or cared for. Author and leadership coach Carey Nieuwhof warns in *Didn't*

*See It Coming* that leaders who focus more on online engagement than face-to-face interactions risk losing the depth that makes ministry meaningful.

Social media is a tool, not a replacement for real relationships. As Nieuwhof puts it, "You can't download intimacy, and you can't manufacture deep trust in a moment. Real relationships take time and presence." Younger generations want leaders who will step out from behind the screen, put down their phones, and invest in them personally, because "likes" don't replace love, and followers don't replace fellowship.

## Generational Divides in Leadership

Generational differences can also make relational leadership challenging. Younger Christians, especially Millennials and Gen Z, tend to value authenticity over authority. They're not as impressed by titles or credentials. They want leaders who are real, who are willing to admit their struggles and walk alongside them. On the other hand, older generations often expect leaders to maintain a sense of formality or distance, which can create tension within the church.

Leaders today have to learn how to navigate these expectations. It's about being flexible enough to connect with people where they are, without losing sight of your core identity as a leader. This might mean listening more than talking, being vulnerable enough to admit when you're wrong, or finding ways to bring generations together through shared experiences.

## Relational Leadership Is About Showing Up

The beauty of relational leadership is that you don't need a perfect plan or endless resources, you just need to show up. It's about being there for the big moments and the small ones, sitting with someone in their pain, and celebrating with them in their joy. It's not flashy, and it doesn't always fit neatly into a job description, but it's what people need the most. When leaders are truly present, it sends a clear message: *You matter.* And let's be honest, sometimes, that message can speak louder than the most powerful sermon or well-crafted strategy ever could.

Relational leadership thrives on the ability to adapt because people aren't all the same. Everyone you lead brings their own story, struggles, and strengths to the table, and as a leader, your role is to meet them where they are, not where you think they should be. Paul Hersey's idea in *The Situational Leader* reminds us that leadership is a dynamic process. It's not about sticking to one approach and expecting it to work for everyone; it's about being in tune with the people around you and adjusting your leadership style to meet their needs in real-time.

This kind of flexibility requires more than awareness, it takes intentionality. It means taking the time to understand what's going on beneath the surface. Is someone's struggle rooted in fear or a lack of confidence? Does someone else need encouragement, or are they ready to be challenged to step out of their comfort zone?

Leaders who practice relational leadership don't assume they know what someone needs, they ask, they listen, and they observe. When you are willing to adapt, you're showing that the person in front of you matters, not for what they do, but for who they are.

For many disillusioned Christians, one of the deepest wounds is feeling like they were valued only for what they could do, not for who they are. Maybe you've felt that before, like the church appreciated you for serving in a ministry or showing up to events but never really saw your heart or struggles.

True relational leadership breaks through that. It says, *I see you, not just what you contribute.* It's recognizing that every person is uniquely created, with a story that deserves to be heard and a soul that needs to be nurtured.

Adaptability allows leaders to look beyond tasks or expectations and connect with the person underneath. It creates space for authenticity, where people feel safe to bring their whole selves—their doubts, their hurts, and their hopes—knowing they won't be reduced to their role or dismissed because of their struggles. For someone who's felt unseen or undervalued, that kind of connection can be life changing.

> *For many disillusioned Christians, one of the deepest wounds is feeling like they were valued only for what they could do, not for who they are.*

The beauty of this approach is that it allows people to feel supported. When a leader adjusts their style to fit where someone is in the moment, it communicates that their unique journey matters. Empathy and discernment reach people in ways no leadership formula ever will. And that's what makes relational leadership not only effective but deeply meaningful for both the leader and the people they're leading.

James Hunter puts it simply in *The World's Most Powerful Leadership Principle*: Leadership finds its purpose in serving others and improving the lives of those you lead. He says, "Leadership is about making the lives of those around you better, not about making your own life easier." That flips the whole idea of leadership on its head, doesn't it?

Relational leadership isn't about what the leader can achieve; it's about what the people being led need. And that means serving others, even when it's inconvenient or messy. It's putting their needs above your own agenda, which is exactly what servant leadership is all about.

For leaders who feel disconnected, it's tempting to think you need to fix everything or have all the answers to start reconnecting. But that's not what relational leadership is about. It's about starting small, taking intentional steps toward building trust and creating space for vulnerability.

And for those who feel disillusioned with the church, it's not the grand gestures that matter most. It's the simple things: a leader who listens without judgment, who leads with humility, and who isn't afraid of having the hard conversations.

Relational leadership isn't about standing above people as an authority figure; it's about walking alongside them as someone who gets it, as someone who's in the same messy, complicated journey of life and faith.

And when we look at Jesus, isn't that exactly how He led?

He didn't rely on programs or policies to connect with people. He showed up in their lives. He walked with His disciples, ate meals with them, laughed with them, and even cried with them. He didn't wait for them to have it all figured out before He invested in them.

That's the kind of leadership that changes lives—not because it's flashy or impressive, but because it's real. That's the kind of leadership the church needs today.

Relational leadership gives us the chance to hit pause, stop being so busy, and refocus on what really matters. Connection begins with presence. It's about choosing connection over control, relationships over routines, and service over self. And as we lean into this, the next step is figuring out how to take all of these ideas and turn them into real, everyday habits that can transform the way we lead, and the lives of the people we're leading.

## Relational Leadership as the Foundation of the Church

Relational leadership is more than a style. It captures the heart of what it means to lead like Christ. It's about stepping into the messiness of people's lives because it's what matters most. Leadership in the church isn't about managing people from a distance or defining success by metrics or programs. It's about reflecting Christ's love through intentional connection and investment in the people you serve.

Francis Schaeffer, in *The Great Evangelical Disaster*, warned about the danger of the church losing its integrity when it prioritizes preserving its systems over embodying the love of Christ. When leaders focus on tasks and structures at the expense of relationships, they may grow in numbers, but the heart of the church—the community—is at risk of becoming hollow.

A church that looks successful on the outside but fails to live out relational love ultimately undermines its message. Leadership that embraces relationships over results restores the church's credibility by living out the gospel in tangible, personal ways.

Leadership is never a one-size-fits-all approach. People are unique, with different struggles, needs, and strengths, and relational leaders adapt to meet those needs where they are. This isn't about micromanaging or trying to solve every problem. Instead, it means being present, attentive, and intentional. That starts with asking thoughtful questions, listening deeply, and responding in ways that build trust and strengthen connection. This kind of flexibility communicates genuine value.

The truth is, relational leadership starts with the leader's own heart. It challenges us to ask hard questions:

Are we prioritizing people over productivity? Are we more focused on outcomes than on connection?

Relational leadership is marked by presence, humility, and a willingness to serve, rather than the need to have all the answers. It's about leading with love, even when it's inconvenient or uncomfortable. When leaders choose this path, they set the tone for the entire church, creating a culture where trust, authenticity, and belonging can flourish.

> *relational leadership starts with the leader's own heart.*

## Takeaways for Relational Leadership

Relational leadership starts with small, intentional steps that create deep connections. Let's unpack each takeaway to show how leaders can integrate these ideas into their daily lives, enriched with stories and historical context to bring them to life.

### 1. Ask More Questions, Give Fewer Instructions

One of the simplest yet most powerful ways to lead relationally is to ask questions that show genuine interest. Questions like, *"What's been on your heart lately?"* or *"How can I support you right now?"* go beyond surface-level interactions and open the door for trust.

Consider Jesus' leadership. In Mark 10:51, when He encountered the blind man Bartimaeus, He didn't assume what the man needed. Instead, He asked, *"What do you want me to do for you?"* In this moment, Jesus wasn't focused on displaying power. He chose instead to give Bartimaeus a voice and show that his needs truly mattered.

Modern leaders can take this approach by creating space for their teams or congregations to express themselves. For example, a pastor might start a meeting by asking, *"What's one challenge you're facing this week?"* rather than jumping straight to tasks. This not only builds relational equity but often reveals deeper needs that would have otherwise gone unnoticed.

This kind of leadership isn't limited to those with a title or a platform. If you have influence in someone's life, you're leading. And how you lead in those everyday moments matters, especially when it comes to walking alongside others in the gospel.

## 2. Be Present in the Everyday Moments

Leadership is more than celebrating big milestones. It's found in consistently showing up during the small, ordinary moments that often matter most. Consider the ministry of John Wesley, a key figure in the Protestant movement. Wesley didn't confine his leadership to pulpits or grand sermons; he made it a point to meet people in their everyday lives.

He traveled on horseback for thousands of miles, often stopping to have personal conversations with individuals, visiting homes, and praying with families. His willingness to be present in the mundane moments of life helped spark a movement rooted in relational connection and spiritual growth.

For church leaders today, this might look like pausing for a five-minute conversation with a congregant after a service or sending a quick text to someone going through a tough time. It could mean showing up for a child's school event or visiting a congregant at their workplace just to say hello. These small, consistent actions build trust and create a sense of belonging.

People tend to remember leaders who show up in the quiet everyday moments, long after the words from the platform have faded. Being present in these everyday moments is a powerful way to demonstrate that people matter, for who they are.

## 3. Adapt Your Leadership to Individual Needs

Paul Hersey, in *The Situational Leader*, makes it clear that effective leadership means being adaptable. People aren't all wired the same, and they're not all in the same season. What works for one person might completely miss the mark for someone else, which is why rigid, one-size-fits-all leadership often falls short.

In a modern context, this could mean recognizing that one team member thrives on encouragement while another responds better to direct challenges. A relational leader takes the time to understand these differences and leads accordingly, creating an environment where people feel supported rather than misunderstood.

## 4. Lead by Serving

Leadership rooted in service is the heart of relational leadership, it's where true influence begins. Jesus made this clear when His disciples were arguing about status and power. Instead of rebuking them, He redefined leadership entirely: "Whoever wants to become great among you must be your servant, and whoever wants to be first must be your slave, just as the Son of Man did not come to be served, but to serve, and to give His life as a ransom for many" (Matthew 20:26-28).

In a world that sees leadership as climbing the ranks, Jesus showed that true greatness comes from humility and sacrifice. He wasn't concerned with titles or recognition. His focus was always on meeting the needs of others. He calls us to the same kind of leadership, not one that seeks to be served, but one that actively serves, sacrifices, and uplifts others.

But not all leadership that appears to be servant-hearted actually is. There's a blind spot many leaders don't realize they have, the difference between serving to lead and leading to serve. True servant leadership isn't about convenience or recognition; it's about character, sacrifice, and a commitment to others, even when there's no personal gain.

The real test of servant leadership isn't how you serve when it's visible or beneficial but how you serve when there's no reward. Great leaders serve whether they are seen or unseen, whether they benefit or not. If your service depends on what you get in return, it's not serving, it's networking. If you only serve when it benefits you, it's not leadership, it's self-promotion. A leader driven by personal gain isn't a servant leader at all—they're a strategic opportunist.

Leading by serving flips the traditional idea of leadership on its head. The heart of leadership is found in the willingness to step into ordinary, difficult moments, not in the pursuit of status or applause. Servant leadership transforms both the leader and the people they serve. It breaks down pride, cultivates empathy, and fosters deeper connections. True leadership is built on character, not convenience.

> A leader driven by personal gain isn't a servant leader at all—they're a strategic opportunist.

Imagine a leader who isn't afraid to roll up their sleeves and join in, someone who carries chairs for an event instead of directing others to do it or takes time to visit the hospital room of a hurting member, even when their schedule is full. These moments speak louder than any sermon because they demonstrate the love of Christ in action. They remind people that their leader isn't above them but with them.

Servant leadership is about impact, not incentives. It's about leading with a heart that asks, *Am I doing this for people or position?* Jesus showed us that leadership isn't about climbing higher; it's about going lower and meeting people in their needs and showing them, they matter.

True servant leadership isn't a duty; it's a privilege. It's a chance to live out the gospel in the most personal way, creating a lasting impact on both those you serve and your own heart. In a world where leadership is often tied to power and prestige, leading by serving is the kind of leadership that truly changes lives.

## 5. Foster a Culture of Authenticity

Authenticity is one of the most powerful tools a leader can use, yet it's often one of the most underutilized. When leaders are willing to be real, sharing their struggles, admitting their mistakes, and being transparent about their journey, it creates an atmosphere where others feel safe to do the same. Vulnerability isn't weakness; it's strength. It tells people, *"I'm not perfect, but I'm walking this road with you."*

Sharing your struggles as a leader doesn't mean airing every personal challenge or putting all your insecurities on display. It means showing people that you're human, that you've wrestled with doubts, faced failures, and still found God's grace to carry you through. Paul modeled this beautifully in 2 Corinthians 12:9-10 when he said, *"I will boast all the more gladly about my weaknesses, so that Christ's power may rest on me."* By admitting his limitations, Paul showed the church that God's strength shines brightest in our weakest moments. For modern leaders, sharing similar stories can break down walls and build bridges, reminding people that they're not alone in their struggles.

When leaders embrace authenticity, it breeds trust—the bedrock of any healthy relationship. Brené Brown, in *Daring Greatly*, writes, *"Vulnerability is the birthplace of connection and the path to the feeling of worthiness."* People gravitate toward leaders who are real, not perfect.

When a leader admits a mistake, it doesn't diminish their authority; it enhances their credibility. It shows they value honesty over image, which creates a culture where others feel they can be honest, too. Over time, this builds relational connection and mutual respect, strengthening the bond between leaders and those they serve.

The benefits of authenticity extend beyond individual relationships; it transforms the culture of an entire church. When leaders lead with vulnerability, they create an environment where people feel safe to open up about their own struggles.

This fosters a deeper community, reduces feelings of isolation, and builds a sense of belonging. Imagine a church where no one feels the need to wear a mask, where people can bring their whole selves, joys, fears, and failures, without fear of judgment. That's what happens when leaders choose authenticity.

For a leader, fostering authenticity might mean sharing a personal story during a sermon, owning up to a misstep in a meeting, or simply saying, *"I don't know, but I'm willing to figure it out with you."* These moments of honesty remind people that their leader is walking the same journey of faith, with all its ups and downs. And that's the kind of leadership that transforms entire communities.

## 6. Evaluate Your Leadership Regularly

Great leaders take the time to step back and reflect on their leadership. Are you leading in a way that values people over productivity? Are you building trust or creating distance? These questions aren't always easy to ask, but they're essential for growth.

The integrity of the church hinges on more than just good preaching or strong programs. It depends on how well we actually live out the love we talk about. When leaders start prioritizing image or activity over real relationships, something gets lost. That's why taking time to regularly reflect and reevaluate is so important. It helps leaders stay grounded in what truly matters and keeps their leadership centered on the relational heart of the gospel.

Practical ways to evaluate leadership might include seeking feedback from trusted mentors, engaging in regular prayer and self-reflection, or even asking your team directly, *"How can I lead you better?"* Honest feedback creates opportunities for growth and helps leaders stay rooted in relational principles.

Relational leadership is about choosing connection over control. By asking questions, being present, adapting to needs, leading by serving, fostering authenticity, and reflecting on your leadership regularly, you can create a culture that mirrors Christ's love and transforms lives.

Strong leaders know they don't have to solve everything. Sometimes the most powerful thing they can do is make room for others to rise. When we choose to walk with people instead of ahead of them, trust is built, transformation takes root, and the church starts to look a lot more like the family God intended it to be.

## The Heartbeat of Leadership

Relational leadership is the heartbeat of the church. It's the difference between a church that thrives and one that simply functions. Programs, strategies, and structures may help organize a ministry, but they will never replace the power of genuine connection.

Jesus transformed lives by entering into people's realities. He called them by name and walked closely with them. That kind of leadership is what the church needs today. True leadership is marked by presence, service, and love, not by position, control, or authority.

It's about leaders who are willing to listen before they instruct, serve before they command, and love before they lead. This is the kind of leadership that retains people, and it restores them. And in a world longing for something real, leaders who prioritize relationships will be the ones who build churches that last.

When leaders lead with love, not image, it changes the culture of the entire church. But that kind of leadership can only thrive when we start redefining what success truly looks like. If we keep measuring success by worldly standards—platforms, performance, and numbers—we'll keep producing leaders who burn out and churches that look busy but feel empty.

If we want a church that reflects the heart of Christ, we need a new lens. We need to talk about success, not how the world defines it, but how Jesus modeled it.

## Chapter 8
# Redefining Success

## How the World Defines Success

Success is a word we throw around all the time, and on the surface, it seems so simple. But when you peel back the layers, you'll find it's loaded with meaning, shaped by our culture, personal dreams, and the values society holds up as important.

In today's world, success often gets defined by things you can measure and show off. It's about landing the big promotion, earning degrees, building a thriving business, or stacking up awards that make others take notice.

From ads to movies to the way we talk about our lives, we're constantly bombarded with the message that success means standing out, rising above the crowd, and proving our worth.

We've been raised in a culture that puts achievement on a pedestal, where doing it all on your own is seen as the gold standard. Think about it: from a young age, we're told to be self-made, to trust ourselves above all else, and to forge our own way. It sounds strong. It sounds admirable. But there's a flip side.

We're so wired to chase independence and chase the next big thing that sometimes we don't even notice how it pulls us away from people. In the hustle to reach goals and prove we're enough, we can end up pushing relationships to the side, trading real connection for constant striving. And honestly, it leaves us more isolated than we realize.

And here's the catch: when success is all about what you can accomplish on the outside, it turns into this never-ending race. You hit one goal—a new job title, a degree, some big win—and instead of feeling full, you just feel the pressure to level up again. Nietzsche called it the "will to power," that constant push for more that never really satisfies. And honestly? It leaves you drained, feeling alone, and wondering why it still feels like something's missing. In this version of success, people often chase appearances while joy, purpose, and what truly matters quietly slip away.

## When Individualism Shapes Ministry

It's easy to see how the world's obsession with measurable success seeps into the church. When we focus on ministry metrics—attendance, budgets, or the number of programs we offer—they can unintentionally turn into benchmarks for comparison. Suddenly, it's not just about faithfully serving where God has called us; it becomes about measuring up to the church down the street. Are their seats fuller? Is their worship team trendier? Is their social media feed more polished? These comparisons create an unspoken competition that no one wants to admit, but everyone feels.

For smaller churches, this pressure can feel overwhelming. Leaders may find themselves questioning their worth or effectiveness because their ministry doesn't look as impressive on the outside. It's exhausting to feel like you're constantly falling short, even when you're pouring your heart into the work God has given you.

This comparison game robs churches of the unique calling God has placed on them. The church with 50 members faithfully discipling its community is no less successful in God's eyes than the megachurch, drawing thousands every week.

Here's where the tension lies: when metrics become the mission, ministry starts to drift. Numbers can tell part of the story, but they don't capture the heart of ministry. Success in the kingdom is measured by faithfulness, not accolades. True purpose in the Church isn't found in competition or self-promotion. It's revealed through transformed lives, relationships grounded in Christ's love, and a steady commitment to the mission God has given us.

When numbers take center stage, the heart of ministry can subtly shift. Programs that should be opportunities for connection may feel like projects to manage, and attendance can overshadow the individual stories that make up those numbers. Milestones like new members and packed events are worth celebrating, but they're also invitations to reflect: *Are we fostering genuine relationships? Are we helping people grow closer to God?* In the end, God's definition of success is rooted in relationships, not results. It's not about bigger rooms; it's about deeper roots.

> when metrics become the mission, ministry starts to drift

When we zero in on what really matters, we start to notice the beauty in the people, not just the numbers. A healthy church isn't about how packed the room is; it's about how deep the relationships go, how people are growing in their faith, and how discipleship is actually happening. Sure, numbers can help us see progress, but real success? That's found in the kind of life change that happens when someone truly experiences God's love. That kind of perspective shifts everything, it challenges us to make sure every event, every plan, and every goal is all about building a community where God's love is real, shared, and lived out day by day.

## The Cost of Performance-Driven Ministry

When churches start chasing the world's version of success, something deeper often gets lost, our soul health. Leaders can get so wrapped up in trying to show results that they slowly start to run dry. They're giving and giving, but inside, they're empty. Eugene Peterson said it best in *The Pastor: A Memoir*, this drift toward performance is "a betrayal of the soul." When ministry becomes about image and outcomes, we start losing the heart behind the calling.

And this isn't just something pastors deal with. The whole church feels it. Big crowds and smooth programs might attract people at first, but if there's no real connection or spiritual depth, that excitement fades, and disillusionment sets in. The scary part? We can have momentum and still miss the mission.

That's why it's so important to redefine what success really looks like. If we're chasing popularity but ignoring relationships, we're building something shaky. But when we lean into discipleship, real community, and the slow, steady work of spiritual transformation, we're building something that lasts. Francis Chan talks about this in *Letters to the Church*, reminding us to resist the pull of flashy models and focus on creating space for deep discipleship and real soul care.

Even the way we celebrate wins says a lot. Are we clapping for lights and hype, or are we honoring the quiet faithfulness of behind-the-scenes prayer, simple kindness, and years of showing up for people? True ministry doesn't always go viral—but it always goes deep. And that's where real growth happens: in the faithful, everyday love of people walking with God and with each other.

## Why This Matters?

The way we define success affects everything; how we live, how we lead, and how we do ministry. If the world's standards shape our idea of success, our churches will start to reflect a results-focused culture. Relationships may feel surface-level, ministry can become a performance, and people might show up at church expecting to consume rather than connect.

But what if we took a step back? What if we asked deeper questions: Is this really the kind of success God calls us to? What would happen if we stopped chasing numbers and started investing in people instead? And how can we redefine success to reflect the kingdom values Jesus taught?

As we dive deeper, we'll explore what it looks like to move away from this performance-driven approach and toward a biblical vision of success. This means celebrating transformation instead of numbers, valuing relationships over recognition, and prioritizing faithfulness above all else.

But before we can embrace this shift, we need to understand how the world's definition of success has shaped us. Recognizing these patterns is eye-opening. It's the first step toward redefining success in a way that honors God and builds His kingdom in lasting, enriching ways.

## What Drives Churches to Chase Numbers?

The pressure to chase numbers in church doesn't appear out of thin air. It's shaped by external expectations, internal ambition, and a culture that constantly pushes us to do more. In a world that applauds measurable results, it becomes easy to assume that high attendance, increased giving, and packed calendars are signs of success. And while those things can reflect growth, they also have the potential to pull our focus away from what truly matters.

What begins as a sincere desire to reach people for Jesus can slowly turn into a hustle for stats and success that looks a lot more like the world than the Kingdom. When that happens, we lose sight of the deeper calling: growing people in Christ, making disciples, and building a real, life-giving community.

Externally, there's a lot of pressure pushing churches to *look* successful. In today's culture, people often judge a church by how big it is or how visible it seems, like it has to prove its worth just to be taken seriously.

But it's not only the outside world. Inside, leaders feel it too. The pressure to produce results can come from all directions, denominational goals, peer comparisons, or just wanting to meet the expectations of the people they serve. And that's where things can get tricky. When churches start borrowing corporate growth strategies just to boost attendance, ministry can quietly take a backseat to marketing.

Yes, numbers can be useful, they show movement and give perspective. But they should never take the place of the deeper work we're called to do: nurturing transformation and building real, lasting relationships. That's where the heart of ministry lives.

## Cultural Influence and Competition

We're living in a world that's all about speed and results. Everywhere you look, it's hustle harder, do more, and get there faster. So it makes sense that churches feel that same pressure to grow quickly, to show numbers, to prove they're "doing well." It's the culture we breathe. Philosopher Charles Taylor talks about how this obsession with control and efficiency often strips away something more important, real connection and depth.

But here's the thing: spiritual growth doesn't work like that. It's not fast. It's not always visible. And it's definitely not something we can manufacture. Paul breaks it down so simply in 1 Corinthians 3:6: *"I planted the seed, Apollos watered it, but God has been making it grow."* In other words, success in the Kingdom isn't about filling seats. It's about changed lives, hearts touched by the love of Jesus, and people growing slowly but deeply in their faith.

Still, we can't ignore how the "bigger is better" mindset sneaks into the church. We're in a consumer-driven culture, and without even realizing it, we start measuring effectiveness the same way businesses do, by how many people show up, how polished the events are, or how trendy the worship feels.

And that can start to twist things. Instead of cheering each other on, churches can slip into quiet competition, worrying about losing people to the church down the street with the better band or the flashier building. Before you know it, ministry becomes marketing. Faithfulness gets pushed aside for appearances. And in all of that noise, the real mission—making disciples and building authentic, Jesus-centered community—can quietly start to disappear.

Social media has a way of turning up the pressure, doesn't it? One scroll through your feed and you're hit with images of packed churches, incredible worship teams, and events that look straight out of a promo video. And while those moments are often real celebrations of what God is doing, they can also quietly mess with your head. For pastors and leaders, those highlight reels can stir up questions like: *Are we doing enough? Are we keeping up? Are we falling behind?* It's a silent comparison game that can shift your focus without you even realizing it.

The problem is, what you're seeing is the surface level. Social media rarely shows the slow, sacred work that happens behind the scenes, the conversations, the mentoring, the healing, the messy but beautiful growth. And when the goal becomes looking relevant instead of being rooted, churches can start drifting.

It's easy to get caught up in chasing what's trendy, mimicking what seems to be working for others, but chasing relevance based on appearance doesn't last. It might draw a crowd, but it won't take people deeper. At the end of the day, what makes the church powerful has everything to do with Jesus and very little to do with presentation.

When churches step back from the noise and focus on real discipleship, spiritual depth, and loving people well, something beautiful happens. They start reflecting the heart of God, a God who doesn't need filters, flashy lights, or perfect stages to move. That's the kind of relevance that actually sticks. Not the kind built on trends, but the kind built on the timeless, life-changing love of Jesus.

## Misaligned Metrics of Success

Success in ministry isn't always about what's seen or celebrated publicly. In fact, some of the greatest victories happen in quiet, unassuming moments that will never make a headline or a social media feed. It's the teenager who, after weeks of doubt, surrenders their heart to Christ in a small group setting. It's the grieving parent who finds a glimmer of peace during a heartfelt prayer. It's the unexpected friendship that forms over a shared meal, offering a connection where there was once loneliness.

These moments might seem small to the world, but in God's eyes, they carry eternal weight. They reflect His heart, a heart that moves in grand gestures and also in steady, faithful love that transforms lives one by one. These quiet moments of impact may never trend, but they are heaven's true milestones.

Unfortunately, the numbers game has crept its way into church leadership, and it's often fueled by the same business mindset we see in the world around us. Everywhere you turn, there are books, conferences, and seminars pushing strategies for growth, marketing tricks, and ways to be more efficient. And to be fair, some of those tools can be helpful. But they can also make ministry feel like a formula: invest time and money, and boom—expect big, visible results.

When we redefine success to celebrate these quiet victories, it changes everything. The focus shifts from impressing others to noticing the beauty in what God is already doing. It's found in the lives touched, the hearts softened, and the seeds of faith quietly taking root. These moments are a reminder that ministry isn't about performance; it's about people. And while the world might overlook them, heaven takes notice. As Jesus said in Luke 15:10, *"There is rejoicing in the presence of the angels of God over one sinner who repents."*

## Fear of Decline and Desire for Recognition

Fear creeps in when numbers dip, attendance falls, giving slows, and suddenly, leaders feel the weight of needing to prove their effectiveness. But success in God's kingdom has never hinged on size or scale. Just ask Gideon. In Judges 7, God instructed him to reduce his army to just 300 men, not to weaken him, but to remind him that victory comes from God's power, not human strategy. That same truth still speaks today: faithfulness matters more than force, and trust always outweighs appearance.

Seasons of decline aren't signs of failure; they can be invitations to return to what matters most. In a world chasing recognition, it's tempting to tie our identity to results, viewing full rooms as confirmation and smaller turnouts as cause for doubt. But real success isn't about applause or optics; it's about obedience and impact, even when the work is hidden.

Yes, wanting to grow and reach more people is a good and godly desire, but when numbers become the goal instead of the fruit, the mission starts to blur. The heartbeat of the Church has never been performance—it's always been people. When we surrender our need to impress and choose instead to invest in transformation, we reflect the true nature of Christ's ministry: steady, faithful, and eternally impactful.

## A Call to Redefine Success

Redefining success in the church means flipping the script. What truly matters in the church isn't measured by attendance or polished programs, but by transformed lives and meaningful relationships. Jesus gave us a totally different picture of what success looks like in the Beatitudes (Matthew 5:3–12). He lifted up values like humility, mercy, purity, and peacemaking, not exactly the kind of stuff that shows up in a performance report.

But that's the point. These things may not be flashy or easy to count, but they show the true heart of God. When a church leans into that kind of model, success looks a lot more like faithfulness,

> The heartbeat of the Church has never been performance—it's always been people.

deep relationships, and genuine love for each other and for the community. That's the kind of impact that lasts.

Let's talk about success. The kind of success that doesn't show up in spreadsheets or Instagram posts but the kind that matters to God. In Matthew 25:35-40, Jesus gives us a powerful picture of what that looks like. He says, *"For I was hungry and you gave me something to eat, I was thirsty and you gave me something to drink, I was a stranger and you invited me in. ... Whatever you did for one of the least of these brothers and sisters of mine, you did for me."*

Think about that for a moment. Success, in God's eyes, isn't about how much we achieve or how impressive our lives look from the outside. It's about how we show up for others: feeding the hungry, welcoming the outsider, caring for those in need. It's about seeing the people around us and meeting them right where they are, with love and compassion.

This kind of success doesn't come with a spotlight. It's not loud or flashy. There's no applause, no viral moment, but it's real. It's rooted in relationship, in quiet impact, and in a love that runs deep. When we start measuring success by how well we love and serve, everything shifts.

But here's the tension: we live in a time where even the most sacred, behind-the-scenes moments can get pulled into the spotlight. Some people, often with good intentions, take these quiet acts of love and post them online to inspire or encourage others. But if we're not careful, we can start using these moments as proof of impact, turning something deeply personal into a public performance. And that was never the point.

True success isn't stage-sized, it's soul-sized. It shows up in the way we reflect Jesus in everyday acts of kindness, prayer, presence, and love. Whether anyone sees it or not, heaven does and that's what truly counts.

Jesus' words in Matthew 25 challenge us to redefine what it means to live a successful life. Living generously means offering our time, our resources, and our hearts with open hands. And the beauty of it is that when we do these small acts of love, we're really serving Him.

A church that focuses on people over performance feels different. The emphasis isn't on numbers, perfect programs, or flawless productions but on creating a space where relationships are valued and faith is nurtured. In this kind of community, every person is seen and celebrated for who they are, made in the image of God. Here, success is found in the quiet yet powerful work of building connections, fostering spiritual growth, and walking alongside one another in authenticity and grace.

In this type of culture, the beauty of connection draws people in. They feel empowered to use their God-given gifts, not out of obligation but with a sense of purpose and belonging. Every small act, whether it's a prayer offered in sincerity, a meal shared with someone in need, or a listening ear given at the right moment, takes on eternal significance.

When success is measured by transformation and relationships, the church becomes a vibrant reflection of God's kingdom. It becomes a refuge for the weary, a source of joy for the broken, and a beacon of hope that radiates far beyond its walls, touching lives in ways that spreadsheets and numbers could never capture.

## How Can Churches Balance Priorities?

Balancing priorities in ministry isn't easy; it takes constant attention and heart checks. It's about staying anchored to the mission, even while being open to different ways of living it out. At the end of the day, the church is here to glorify God, make disciples, and show His love to the world. But with all the pressure around us, whether we're trying to grow, manage resources, or meet expectations, it's easy to get distracted or feel stretched too thin. Finding balance means continually returning to the "why" behind everything the church does.

One of the best ways to stay balanced in ministry is by going back to the core values, often. What does the church believe about discipleship, community, worship, and outreach? Those aren't just nice words on a wall; they should guide every decision. When something new comes up, it helps to ask, "Does this line up with who we are and what we're called to do?" That kind of filter keeps the church from getting sidetracked by things that look exciting on the surface but don't really fit the mission. Staying rooted in your values brings clarity and keeps the focus right where it belongs, on what God has actually called your church to do.

It also takes prayer and honest reflection. In what some consider as the hustle of church life, it's easy to get caught up in doing more—more events, more meetings, more activity—without asking if it's actually helping people grow. But Jesus showed us a better way. Even with crowds pressing in, He stepped away to pray (Luke 5:16). Churches today can follow that same rhythm, slowing down enough to ask the hard questions: *Are we really making space for discipleship, or just keeping busy?* That pause to seek God's direction makes all the difference, it keeps ministry Spirit-led and truly impactful.

And here's the truth: no church is meant to do it all. Trying to copy someone else's model or meet every single need can wear a church out fast. Instead of stretching too thin, churches should lean into what they're uniquely gifted to do. Whether it's building deep relationships, developing powerful discipleship, or meeting specific needs in the community, there's strength in focus. Doing fewer things with excellence instead of everything with mediocrity not only protects against burnout, it builds a lasting legacy of faithfulness and effectiveness, staying fully aligned with God's mission.

## What Are the Practical Steps for Redefining Success?

Redefining success in the church begins with a change in the way we think, moving away from chasing outward markers of growth and focusing instead on the real, lasting impact of internal transformation. It's not about throwing out metrics entirely, but about rethinking what they represent and placing the spotlight on what truly matters: lives being changed by the power of the gospel.

1. **Measure What Matters**

    Rather than relying on attendance or donations as the main markers of success, churches can look for new ways to measure spiritual growth. How many people are actively engaging in discipleship? Are lives being transformed, both personally and spiritually? Is the congregation showing genuine love and care for one another? These kinds of questions shift the focus from numbers to impact, highlighting what truly lies at the heart of ministry.

    o **Define Spiritual Growth** - Clarify what growth looks like (e.g., deeper prayer, active discipleship, service, or displaying the fruit of the Spirit).

- **Track Engagement Over Attendance** - Monitor small group participation, volunteer involvement, and mentorship connections.

- **Assess Community Impact** - Measure outreach efforts: meals served, families helped, or partnerships formed.

- **Gather Feedback** - Use simple surveys or conversations to ask about spiritual growth and connection.

2. **Celebrate Stories of Transformation**

   Churches should take time to celebrate personal stories of growth, healing, and restoration. When someone shares how they've encountered God's love through the church, it brings the true purpose of ministry into focus. These testimonies serve as powerful reminders—for both the congregation and church leaders—that real success isn't about filling seats but about transforming lives.

   - **Create Testimony Moments** – Dedicate time during services or small groups for members to share personal testimonies of growth and healing.

   - **Document Stories** – Record written and video testimonies for newsletters, websites, or social media to inspire and encourage others.

   - **Incorporate Stories in Ministry** – Use testimonies in sermons, leadership meetings, and small group discussions as powerful reminders of God's work.

3. **Invest in Relationships**

   Redefining success means creating a culture where people truly feel valued. This can start with training leaders and volunteers to practice empathy, active listening, and genuine hospitality, making sure every person feels like they belong. A thriving church grows through strong relationships where people support and encourage one another in their walk with God, far more than through impressive events or packed calendars.

- o **Train Leaders in Relational Ministry** – Offer workshops to teach empathy, active listening, and hospitality to leaders and volunteers.

- o **Foster Welcoming Spaces** – Create informal gathering areas and use greeters or connectors to make everyone feel valued.

- o **Recognize and Appreciate Individuals** – Celebrate personal milestones like birthdays or service anniversaries to show people they matter.

4. **Focus on Faithfulness, Not Results**

Paul reminds us in 1 Corinthians 3:6, "I planted the seed, Apollos watered it, but God has been making it grow." This is a freeing truth for churches, letting go of the pressure to produce big results and focusing instead on being faithful to their calling, whether it's mentoring a small group, sharing a meal with the community, or simply praying with someone in need, every act of service matters deeply in God's kingdom, even if it doesn't grab attention or make the headlines.

- o **Encourage Small Acts of Service** – Highlight simple, intentional ways to serve, like mentoring, prayer groups, or meal preparation.

- **Celebrate Faithful Effort** – Recognize behind-the-scenes contributors and long-term volunteers with appreciation events or a personal thank-you.

- **Avoid Over-scheduling** – Regularly evaluate programs and focus on those producing genuine spiritual fruit over busyness.

5. **Create a Culture of Rest**

   Focusing too much on numbers can lead to burnout for both leaders and members. Redefining success means building a culture that values rest and sustainability. Encourage leaders to take sabbaticals, empower volunteers to set healthy boundaries, and remind everyone to prioritize their spiritual health over endless busyness. When a church embraces rest, it creates space for people to serve with joy and energy, ensuring the ministry thrives for the long haul.

   - **Model Rest from Leadership** – Encourage leaders to take breaks, sabbaticals, and share the importance of rest with the congregation.

   - **Establish Healthy Boundaries** – Ensure volunteers and leaders have manageable schedules with regular rotations.

   - **Celebrate Rest** – Organize church-wide rest days, retreats, or reflection moments to emphasize renewal and balance.

When the church redefines success, it leans more fully into its true mission and lives it out with greater depth. The true mission of the church has always been about people: leading them to Christ, walking alongside them in discipleship, and equipping them to share God's love with others.

Shifting the focus from numbers to relationships doesn't make the church smaller, it actually makes the impact deeper and more meaningful. It brings us back to what really matters: people over performance, depth over display, souls over stats.

It's a shift that turns the church from a place of production into a place of renewal. A space where people encounter grace, grow in their faith, and experience love that actually changes them. But leaning into that kind of transformation means letting go of our obsession with quick results. It means trusting God's timeline, not ours.

The world is all about fast wins and flashy success, but God's kingdom works differently. It's slow, steady, and often invisible, like seeds growing underground. The real impact shows up in those quiet, sacred moments that ripple through lives and communities over time.

There's tension here, we feel it. Because the way Jesus measured success is so different from what we see around us. He wasn't chasing crowds or trying to impress anyone. He poured into people, lifted up the overlooked, and always chose faithfulness over fame. That's not the easy road, but it's the one that leads to real purpose, the kind that reflects God's heart.

And as we redefine what success really means—anchoring ourselves in relationships, faithfulness, and genuine transformation—we start to realize something big: culture is everything. It's the atmosphere where all of this either takes root or dies out. Without a healthy culture, even the best ideas or intentions won't last. And sometimes, it takes a little heartbreak to help us see how much that culture really matters.

# Chapter 9
# Sustaining Relational Church Culture

I'll never forget the moment I realized how much culture really matters. Not in theory. Not as a leadership concept. I mean in real life, when the atmosphere we create fails to catch someone who's quietly falling apart. It didn't happen during a powerful sermon or in a big vision meeting. It happened on an ordinary morning, in a room full of people I cared about, when someone who always seemed so full of life was suddenly gone.

It was just after Christmas. The office had been filled with excitement during our holiday party. There were cookies on every table, music playing softly in the background, and laughter in every corner. That was the last time we were all together before leaving for Christmas break. And right in the middle of it all was Evelyn.

Evelyn was the kind of person who lit up every room she walked into. She had this gift of pulling people in and making them feel seen. Her laugh was unforgettable, the kind that made everyone else start laughing too. That night, she floated from group to group, cracking jokes, grabbing extra dessert for someone, making sure no one felt left out.

When the party wrapped up, we hugged and said our Merry Christmas goodbyes. Everyone left with full hearts and plans for family time. It felt like a good night.

Two weeks later, we came back to work and gathered for our usual morning huddle. People were trading stories about their holidays. Some had traveled, some stayed local, and more than one person admitted to eating way too much pie. It felt like we were easing back into the rhythm again.

But something felt off. Our manager had not shown up yet, which was unusual. He was always the first one in the room. After about fifteen minutes, he finally walked in. His head was low, his steps were slow, and his eyes looked heavy like he hadn't slept.

We all went quiet. He stood there trying to speak, but the words just wouldn't come. Then, completely overwhelmed, he started to cry. Not a quiet tear or two, but a full, broken kind of cry that made everyone stop. A few of us started tearing up just from watching him, while others sat frozen, unsure of what was happening.

After a few painful moments, he finally spoke.

"She's gone. Evelyn is gone."

For a second, no one understood what he meant. I looked around and realized her empty chair. I asked quietly, "Where's Evelyn?"

He took a deep breath and said the words I'll never forget.

"She took her life."

The room went still. The shock hit all at once. Evelyn, the one who laughed the loudest, the one who made others feel like they belonged, was no longer with us.

That was the moment everything changed. That was when I realized how much the atmosphere we create matters. Not just how we lead, but how we see each other. How we check in. How we slow down enough to notice what someone might be hiding behind a smile.

And I've carried that moment with me ever since.

None of us knew the pain Evelyn had been carrying. Behind her bright smile and endless energy was a heartbreak most of us never saw coming. Just a year earlier, she had lost her brother to cancer. Two months before Christmas, her fifteen-year marriage ended in a devastating divorce.

Her parents lived far away, across the country, and that left her feeling isolated. But you never would have known. She kept all of it to herself, hiding her hurt behind laughter and kindness.

When I heard the news, I broke. And I wasn't the only one. Tears filled the room. Some people sat in stunned silence, others wept openly. But underneath the grief, I felt something heavier. Guilt. Shame. Not the kind you shake off after a few hours. It settled in like a weight, thick and suffocating.

I had always seen myself as someone who connects with people. Someone who notices when something feels off. I took pride in that. It wasn't just what I did, it was how I understood my place in the world. But that day, all of that felt like a lie. I started to question everything. How did I miss it? How could I spend so much time with someone, work alongside them every day, and not see what they were holding inside?

Losing Evelyn changed me. It's hard to put it all into words, but at the very least, it made one thing crystal clear. We have to be more intentional with our relationships. Not just friendly. Not just polite. But deeply present. We have to create spaces where people feel safe enough to be real about what they're going through.

It forced me to look closely at my own relationships and the kind of environment I've been helping to create. Whether at work, at home, or in the church, culture is made up of everyday interactions. The way we listen. The way we follow up. The way we check in, even when everything seems fine.

This was a wake-up call. It reminded me that culture shapes the depth and honesty of our relationships. And the way we build that culture determines whether people feel seen, valued, and safe enough to open up. What matters most is being intentional in the way we love and lead. Because sometimes, it's the atmosphere we create that makes all the difference.

## What Is Culture, and Why Does It Matter?

Think of culture like the soil in a garden. No matter how strong the seeds of discipleship are, they need the right kind of soil to grow deep roots and bear fruit. A church's culture is that soil. It's what shapes how people connect, how they grow together, and how they live out their faith as a community.

You can have all the right systems in place—great programs, a solid leadership structure, and a packed calendar—and still miss the mark if the underlying atmosphere isn't right. Culture can be difficult to define because it's more about what you feel than what you see. It's the unspoken norms, behaviors, and atmosphere that shape every interaction.

Psychologists and sociologists often describe culture as the "invisible hand" that guides behavior within a group. Studies on organizational behavior, like those by Edgar Schein, emphasize that culture is formed through shared values, repeated practices, and collective attitudes. Schein's work on organizational culture highlights how it becomes the foundation for decision-making, conflict resolution, and overall morale. This explains why a church's culture influences everything from how people interact to whether they feel truly connected.

Most people don't notice culture because it's always there in the background, like the air we breathe, it's easy to ignore until something doesn't feel right. Culture is defined by what we live out daily, not what we write in a mission statement. It influences everything, often without us realizing it, which is why identifying it requires intentional reflection and honesty about what's really happening beneath the surface.

Culture is the heartbeat of a church. It's the way things really feel when you walk into the room. It's in the way people greet each other, how they handle tough conversations, and how they show love to anyone who walks through the doors. Research in psychology, such as Maslow's hierarchy of needs, supports this by highlighting how belonging and connection are fundamental human needs. A welcoming culture taps into this need, creating a sense of safety and acceptance that encourages people to engage and grow.

Building a healthy church culture begins with being intentional. You can feel it in the little things. It doesn't require anything complicated. Most of the time, it's the small, thoughtful gestures that make the biggest impact. A genuine smile, someone stepping in to help without being asked, or a kind word at the right time can begin to break down walls people carry with them.

Walking into church for the first time can be overwhelming. Some people come with past hurt. Others show up feeling uncertain or guarded. But when the environment feels warm and personal, those fears start to settle. Even something as simple as feeling noticed can shift everything. People don't need to be wowed, they need a space to feel safe enough to be real, not pressured to perform.

That kind of atmosphere needs to carry through the rest of the church, not just the entryway. Culture becomes real when people have meaningful spaces to connect. It might be a small group, a shared meal, or a one-on-one conversation during the week. These are the moments where relationships grow, trust deepens, and people begin to feel known and supported.

This is what helps a church move from being a place people visit to a place they belong.

At its core, culture is about what it's *really like* to be part of the community. More than the official mission statement or website copy, it's what people experience week after week. Is it welcoming? Does it feel real? Are relationships genuine, or do people feel like they're on the outside looking in?

Samuel Chand says it well in his book *Cracking Your Church's Culture Code*: "Culture—not vision—is the most powerful factor in any organization." What he's getting at is this: you can have the best plans and goals, but if the culture doesn't match, it won't go anywhere. Culture is what makes the vision come alive.

And here's why this matters so much: Culture affects *everything*. A healthy church culture draws people closer, helps them feel safe, and makes room for honesty and growth. But an unhealthy culture? It pushes people away, creates tension, and keeps the church from living out its calling to reflect God's love.

In a church that's serious about relationships, culture becomes the space where people truly connect. It's where spiritual growth moves from merely learning about God to living life with others in a way that shows His love. When gratitude, truth, and care are at the center of the culture, they sustain the church and help it thrive.

## The Power of Intentional Culture

Culture is never an accident. Whether we realize it or not, every church already has a culture. It's the sum of all the unspoken norms, attitudes, and behaviors that shape how the community operates. But without intentional effort, culture can drift away from what's healthy, leading to misaligned values, relational dysfunction, and even burnout.

When culture is left to chance, unhealthy patterns can take root. Gossip, cliques, or an emphasis on performance over relationships can quietly undermine the church's mission. Misaligned values, where a church says it values connection but doesn't prioritize spaces for it, leave people feeling disillusioned or disconnected. Even worse, unchecked relational dysfunction can lead to burnout, where people feel overworked and undervalued, seeing the church as another obligation instead of a place of rest and growth.

When a church doesn't build culture on purpose, everyone feels it. People can start to feel overlooked or left out, especially when relationships aren't a priority. Instead of feeling connected and excited to be part of something, they pull back. Visitors pick up on it too. They might sense that they don't really belong, or that there's this unspoken "in-crowd" vibe that makes it hard to settle in.

And it's not only those inside the church who notice. Even outsiders can spot the cracks when gossip, cliques, or a lack of care start to drown out the message of love the church is meant to share. Without a clear and healthy culture, church can start to feel more like a place of pressure than a place of hope. People walk in looking for grace and walk out feeling judged or forgotten. That's why culture matters so much. It's what helps turn a church into a place where people feel lifted, valued, and inspired to grow.

## Creating Irresistible Environments

Andy Stanley introduces the idea of "irresistible environments" in *Deep and Wide*—spaces designed to draw people in, where they feel welcomed and comfortable, regardless of where they are on their spiritual journey. For Stanley, an irresistible environment isn't about flashy production or perfection; it's about creating a place where people sense they belong before they believe.

Welcoming spaces are where real relationships begin. When people feel safe, they're more likely to open up, build trust, and grow in their faith. A church that makes approachability a priority is sending a clear message: you belong here, just as you are. And that message isn't only for visitors. It reminds everyone that this is a place where relationships matter and where people come first.

Leaders play a big role in setting that tone. Sometimes, connection gets blocked by things that are easy to overlook—like not following up with guests or creating an atmosphere that feels too formal or closed off. Instead, leaders can be intentional about building spaces that reflect God's grace in a real and visible way. When the environment feels thoughtful, kind, and genuine, people are naturally drawn in. That's when community starts to feel real, and relationships have room to grow.

## Building a Culture Where People Feel Valued

Creating a culture where people feel truly valued starts with how leaders and volunteers see their role. The goal is more than getting things done. It's to be present and make every moment matter. When someone is greeted with genuine warmth, when their name is remembered, or when someone notices they're new, it speaks volumes. It tells them they're seen and that they belong. Those small, intentional acts go a long way in helping people feel connected from the very beginning.

Sometimes, without meaning to, we create a gap in how we serve. We step in to help, but we end up doing things for people instead of doing things with them. It usually comes from a sincere desire to bless others or make their experience easier. But over time, that approach can leave people feeling like observers instead of active participants. It can make them feel like they're on the outside of what's happening, rather than part of the team. And when that happens, we miss out on the ownership, creativity, and relationships that grow when people build together.

Jesus showed us a different way. He invited His disciples into the journey, teaching them, walking with them, and eventually empowering them to carry the mission forward. In Mark 6, He gave them authority and sent them out two by two. That moment reflected something deeper. It reflected trust and genuine partnership.

*When we choose to build together, we remind each other that the mission is shared.*

When we build for others, even with the best intentions, it can sometimes send the message that they're only there to receive. But when we build with others, something powerful shifts. People begin to see their own value. Their gifts come alive. Their voices matter. And they start to take ownership of what's being created.

This mindset is what helps build a healthy, sustainable church culture. One where people actively take part in shaping the vision, not simply showing up to support it. It's a big difference to say, "Here's what we made for you," versus saying, "Let's build this together."

With everything pulling people in different directions these days—burnout, distractions, and a culture that encourages doing life alone—this kind of shared approach isn't optional. It's necessary. When we choose to build together, we remind each other that the mission is shared. We stop carrying things on our own, and we start becoming a movement where every person has a place, every gift has value, and every heart is engaged.

## Diagnosing Cultural Challenges

Every church has its challenges when it comes to culture. Even with the best intentions, certain habits or attitudes can creep in and quietly chip away at the community you're trying to build. These are the unspoken barriers that keep people from truly connecting, and they're often hard to spot until the damage is already done. Addressing these challenges requires honesty, reflection, and a willingness to confront uncomfortable truths about what's really happening beneath the surface.

Addressing cultural challenges isn't easy. In fact, it's often avoided altogether. Why? Because it's uncomfortable. Calling out issues like gossip, cliques, or resistance to change means confronting behaviors that people might not even realize are problematic. It means shining a light on areas that we'd rather keep hidden, and let's face it, nobody likes conflict. For some, it feels easier to sweep things under the rug and hope they resolve on their own. But here's the truth: they never do. Ignoring cultural toxins doesn't make them disappear; it just lets them grow.

Sometimes, complacency plays a role. People might think, *This is just how things are,* or *It's not that bad.* They settle for "good enough" because they don't realize how much better it could be. And then there's a lack of awareness. Sometimes the issues are so ingrained in the culture that they feel normal, like part of the air we breathe. But even if the problems feel invisible, their impact is very real, creating tension, disconnection, and a culture that holds people back from thriving.

The good news is that these hurdles can be overcome. It starts with a willingness to face the uncomfortable. Leaders and members alike need to commit to honesty, even when it's hard. Ask the questions that matter: *Where are we falling short? What's really happening beneath the surface?* And then listen without defensiveness or excuses. When these conversations are approached with humility and grace, they open the door to real change.

From there, take one small step forward. You don't have to fix everything overnight, but you do need to start somewhere. Maybe it's addressing one specific behavior, like gossip, and replacing it with a culture of encouragement. Or maybe it's creating a space where people can safely voice their concerns. The first step is always the hardest, but it's also the most important, because it sets the tone for what's to come. The process may be uncomfortable, but the result—a healthy, thriving culture—is more than worth it.

Some of the most damaging barriers are the ones no one talks about. Gossip, for instance, might seem harmless at first, but it can destroy trust and create an atmosphere where people feel unsafe and vulnerable. Then there are cliques, those tight-knit groups that can make others feel like outsiders. And let's not forget the unspoken rules, those invisible expectations about how things are done or who's included, that hold back growth and discourage new ideas. If these barriers go unchecked, they create a culture where people feel disconnected, undervalued, or worse, unwelcome.

In *Cracking Your Church's Culture Code*, Samuel Chand talks about "cultural toxins" that hold churches back. These can be anything from resistance to change to a tolerance for negative behaviors like gossip or passive-aggressiveness. His advice? Don't ignore these issues. Ask the hard questions: What's creating tension? Where are people feeling frustrated or disengaged? Often, the answers to these questions will point to the toxic behaviors that need to be addressed. Remember, whatever is allowed, even passively, will eventually define the culture. Leaders must step up and actively root out what doesn't belong, setting the tone for the kind of environment the church should reflect.

Shaping culture isn't the sole responsibility of leaders. Everyone in the church plays a role. Even those who aren't in official leadership positions can make a big difference. It happens when someone chooses to model grace, speaks up with kindness, or takes time to build real, spirit-led connections with others. When both leaders and members come together, with leaders guiding the way and setting the tone and members stepping in to live it out, a church can begin to move forward. Healing can happen. Trust can be rebuilt. And what once felt broken can start to feel whole again.

Van Moody, in *The People Factor*, talks a lot about the relational side of culture. Issues like broken trust, poor communication, and fear of vulnerability can quietly eat away at the foundation of any church community. It's hard to build strong, purpose-filled relationships if people are afraid to be real with each other. If there's no trust or safety, connection breaks down.

That's why creating an environment built on empathy and accountability matters so much. Healthy relationships are at the heart of a strong church culture. When people feel safe to share, when they know they're not alone, and when they feel supported as they grow, everything begins to shift. The entire church becomes stronger, more connected, and more united. And that kind of culture is where real transformation begins.

## Tools for a Healthier Culture

So, how do you actually address these challenges? It starts with listening. Take time to ask honest, open-ended questions about what's really going on. What's working? What's not? Sometimes, the most powerful insights come when you're willing to listen without getting defensive.

Along with that, pay attention to what's happening between the lines. What's the tone in the room before and after gatherings? Are certain groups dominating? Are issues being swept under the rug instead of being addressed?

Creating safe spaces for dialogue is also key. Whether it's a small group discussion or a focus group, providing a place where people can share their thoughts without fear of judgment can uncover barriers you didn't even realize were there. Once those issues are brought into the open, it's important to talk clearly about what the church stands for. Values like honesty, kindness, and respect need to be named and lived out. People need to hear about them, and they need to see them in action, especially from those leading the way.

When problems like gossip or cliques do come up, we cannot ignore them. They need to be addressed with grace but also with courage. Let people know that protecting the church's relational culture is a priority.

Finally, leaders and members both need the right tools to build stronger relationships. Training in conflict resolution, communication, and emotional intelligence can make a huge difference in creating a healthier culture. It's important not to avoid conflict. It doesn't just go away. In fact, it grows, takes control, and starts to dictate the direction of relationships, leadership, and even the culture itself. If you don't manage conflict, it will manage you.

When you take time to really look at the cultural challenges and start working through them, you're doing more than solving problems. You're creating space for a healthier, more connected church. It's not always easy, but it matters. A culture built on trust, honesty, and genuine care shapes the experience for those inside. It also shows the outside world what it looks like when a community is built on God's love.

## Building and Sustaining a Relational Church Culture

Building a healthy, relational church culture doesn't happen in a day. It takes time, care, and a steady commitment. Culture isn't something you fix once and move on from. It's something you keep shaping, day by day. Just like tending a garden, it needs regular attention to stay healthy and full of life. The most important thing is staying committed for the long run. When you keep the bigger picture in mind, it becomes easier to focus on steady growth rather than rushing to see quick results.

Leadership expert Samuel Chand talks a lot about how culture is built through consistency and intentional effort. It doesn't just fall into place. It takes purpose and clarity to align the church's values, behaviors, and decisions with what Scripture teaches. He encourages leaders to regularly pause and ask, "Does this reflect the heart of Christ?" When leaders are willing to keep asking those questions and adjusting where needed, they help shape a culture where people can truly grow, both in faith and in relationships.

Holding on to a strong culture also means learning how to balance two important things. On one hand, you want to meet people where they are. On the other, you want to encourage them to keep growing. A healthy culture does both. It creates an atmosphere that feels warm and welcoming, while also inviting people to go deeper in their walk with God. When that balance is in place, no one feels left behind or pushed too hard. It becomes a place where both new believers and seasoned disciples can find room to grow.

*A healthy church culture makes space for more than surface-level connections.*

At the core of it all are real, meaningful relationships. A healthy church culture makes space for more than surface-level connections. It creates an environment where people feel safe enough to be honest about what they're walking through. That kind of openness builds trust. And trust is what turns a crowd into a family. When people feel free to share their struggles, their hopes, and their questions, something powerful happens. Without that depth, relationships stay shallow, and the church misses out on the beauty of true community.

## Keeping the Vision Alive

Keeping this kind of culture going starts with a clear and shared vision. Everyone, from leaders to regular members, needs to understand what kind of community they're helping build and why it matters. That shared vision gives the church focus. It helps everyone move in the same direction with the goal of creating real, authentic relationships that reflect the heart of God. Communication plays a big part in this. There need to be regular opportunities to talk about the culture, celebrate what's going well, and address anything that needs attention. Honest conversations build trust and help the whole church stay engaged in the process.

But how do we make sure the vision becomes more than just an idea? It's one thing to talk about building a relational culture. It's something else to keep it alive in a way that keeps people connected, growing, and moving together. This is where intentional practices make all the difference.

One simple but powerful practice is something called a Culture Check-in. These are regular moments, usually once a quarter, where the church pauses to reflect and realign. During these times, leaders create space for open conversation with questions like, "Are new people feeling welcomed?" "Are there people feeling disconnected right now?" The goal isn't to criticize. It's to listen, to grow, and to make sure no one is falling through the cracks.

These check-ins offer leaders real insight into what's working and where more support might be needed. More importantly, they send a strong message that everyone's experience matters. When you create space for people to share stories, give feedback, and speak honestly, the culture grows stronger. It doesn't stay strong because of assumptions or routines. It stays strong because people are choosing to show up, speak up, and stay connected to the vision of being a community that reflects the love of Christ.

## The Role of Consistency, Adaptability, and Leadership in Culture

Consistency is another key element. A healthy culture is reinforced through regular practices that reflect its values, like small group gatherings, acts of service, or intentional opportunities for connection. These practices remind people of what matters most and provide tangible ways to live out the church's mission. Leadership has a particularly important role in this area. When leaders embody the culture—living out its values in their interactions and decisions—it sets the tone for the entire community. People are more likely to follow when they see the culture genuinely modeled by those they trust.

Being adaptable is just as important as being consistent. As the church grows and the world shifts around us, the culture has to be flexible enough to adjust while still holding firm to what matters most. That kind of adaptability helps keep the church healthy and life-giving, no matter what changes come our way. Real impact comes from paying attention to what people need while staying anchored in biblical truth, not from chasing every trend.

Creating a relational church culture takes time. It doesn't happen overnight, and it definitely takes effort. But it's worth it. When that kind of culture is in place, the church becomes a place where people feel seen, known, and loved. It becomes a space where faith grows deeper and relationships reflect the love of Christ in real ways. This kind of environment draws people in. Whether they've been walking with God for years or are just starting to ask questions, they can sense that what's happening is real. And that kind of culture always points back to the heart of God.

## Modern Challenges to Relational Culture

Creating a relational church culture sounds amazing in conversation, but living it out is a whole different story. It takes work. Life is busy, people are carrying a lot, and the world moves fast. All of that can put pressure on even the strongest communities. Things like generational disconnect or the nonstop pace of everyday life can slowly chip away at the connection churches work so hard to build. The encouraging part is that none of these challenges are permanent. With intentional effort and care, things can shift. Even a culture that feels like it's drifting can be restored.

One of the biggest obstacles churches face is the gap between generations. It can sometimes feel like older and younger people are speaking different languages. Older members may feel like their stories, experience, or traditions no longer matter. At the same time, younger members may feel like their ideas are dismissed or that their voice isn't needed. If no one addresses these tensions, the distance keeps growing.

Bridging that gap starts with bringing people together on purpose. It means creating spaces where different generations can talk, listen, and learn from one another. When older members share their stories and offer mentorship, while also staying open to the fresh ideas of younger voices, something powerful happens. You start to see mutual respect form. Moments of laughter, shared wisdom, and collaboration begin to take the place of frustration or misunderstanding. Planning gatherings that blend the richness of tradition with the energy of new ideas can give everyone something to connect over. Little by little, that sense of "us and them" fades away, and what begins to form instead is a real sense of family.

Then there's the pace of life. That constant go, go, go. Most people aren't avoiding relationships because they don't care. They're just exhausted. Between work, school, family, and everything in between, it can feel like there's barely enough energy to show up, let alone build something meaningful with others. And honestly, church events, as good as they might be, can sometimes add more pressure instead of offering rest.

So maybe it's time to ask some honest questions. Are we creating space for people to connect in a real way, or are we simply filling their time with more activity? Churches can be intentional about simplifying the calendar and focusing on what helps people breathe again. Sometimes that means choosing fewer things and doing them with more care. It's also about modeling rest and reminding people that relationships need room to grow. When the pace slows down, people show up differently. They become more present. And when that happens, real connection has the space to take root.

## Identifying and Restoring a Church Culture in Decline

Sometimes, the challenges run deeper, and the culture of a church starts to feel...off. Maybe there's a heaviness in the atmosphere or a sense that people are just going through the motions. Maybe trust has been broken, or there's tension no one wants to name. Whatever it is, the first step to fixing it is to face it. Ask the hard questions: *What's not working? Where are people feeling frustrated or left out?* And here's the hard part, listen. Really listen. Even when the answers are uncomfortable, they're the starting point for healing.

Restoring a struggling culture starts with creating space for honesty and reflection. Leadership has to model vulnerability by owning their part in what went wrong and inviting the community into the process of change. It means revisiting the church's values, clarifying what matters most, and setting a renewed vision for what a healthy culture should look like. As Brené Brown emphasizes in her work on vulnerability and leadership, creating an atmosphere where people feel safe to share openly is essential for trust to be rebuilt. Restoration goes beyond fixing problems, it's about rebuilding trust, fostering unity, and creating an atmosphere where relationships can thrive again.

Restoring a struggling culture isn't something leaders can, or should, do alone. A healthy church culture really starts to grow when everyone feels like they're part of it. That's why it's so important to involve the whole congregation. When people know their voice matters and they have something valuable to contribute, everything begins to shift. The conversation moves from pointing fingers to linking arms. It's no longer about what others need to fix, it becomes, what can we build together? That kind of shared mission, rooted in trust and teamwork, is what brings healing and breathes new life into the church.

One really effective way to get the whole church involved is by creating space for honest conversation through open forums or workshops. These moments are more than just meetings. They're chances for people to share what they've experienced, what concerns them, and what they're hoping for in the future. When leaders step into these spaces with humility and a willingness to listen, something powerful happens. They're not there to argue or explain things away. They're there to learn. These gatherings often help uncover things that might have stayed hidden; barriers, habits, or hurts that need attention. And when people see their voices being heard and their input making a difference, it builds trust and reminds everyone that they're part of shaping the future.

Prayer is also a huge part of this. Restoring culture takes more than good ideas or strategy. It requires a spiritual journey that needs

God's wisdom and direction every step of the way. Making space for prayer as a church—whether that's during services, in small groups, or through special gatherings—unites the whole body around a common purpose. It's a way of saying together, "We want what God wants for this place." When prayer is at the center, people are reminded that this is more than trying to fix problems. It's about aligning hearts with what God is doing.

The real change begins when the church moves as one. Not just from the top down, but side by side. Leaders help guide the way, but the entire church has a role to play. Culture is shaped when people take ownership, when they speak honestly, when they pray together, and when they act with intention. That kind of shared responsibility is what creates lasting momentum. It may not always feel easy, but it's sacred work, and it leaves an impact that can ripple through generations.

You may not see results overnight, but you will start to feel the difference. People will begin to show up more fully as they bring more than their presence, offering their attention, energy, and heart. The conversations will shift. They'll feel more open and more personal. People will stick around after service to talk and catch up. Volunteer teams will feel more united and energized. And guests will walk in and sense something different. They may not know exactly what it is, but they'll feel it. A warmth. A welcome. A sense that they belong.

Patrick Lencioni talks about this in *The Advantage*. He points out that healthy organizations are built on trust, clarity, and a shared sense of purpose. These are the kinds of qualities that make a community thrive.

As you walk this out, keep checking in with your people. Ask questions that matter. Are people feeling more connected? Is trust growing? Are we hearing new stories of people finding a home here? Use both formal and informal moments to listen well and stay open to feedback. A culture that's healing is one where people feel seen, where they feel safe to speak up, and where they feel excited to be part of what's happening.

This kind of restoration takes time, but it's worth every bit of effort. Because when a church gets this right, people experience deep transformation. Relationships reflect God's love, and hope begins to shape the atmosphere of the entire community.

## The Legacy of Relational Culture

> *A healthy, relational culture is the foundation for everything else.*

Culture is what holds everything together. Programs come and go, strategies shift, and even buildings change, but the culture of a church is what truly sustains it. It's the atmosphere where discipleship grows deep roots and where community becomes more than a buzzword. A healthy, relational culture is the foundation for everything else. It keeps people connected to God and one another long after the events and sermons are over. A church culture rooted in this kind of unity helps make sure no one is left behind.

Culture has the power to become a lasting legacy. The way we invest in relationships today shapes the church of tomorrow. When love and genuine connection are woven into the fabric of the church, they create a strong foundation that continues to impact lives long after we're gone. This kind of culture creates space for future leaders, families, and new believers to grow, feel at home, and step into their purpose. Small, intentional acts of care build something meaningful over time. Jesus captured this in *Matthew 5:16 when He said, "Let your light shine before others, that they may see your good deeds and glorify your Father in heaven."*

The legacy of a relational culture isn't built on having everything figured out. It's built on the way we make room for others to be honest, how we love them through the mess, and how we keep pointing each other back to Jesus. When that becomes the rhythm of a church, something powerful happens. Lives begin to change, relationships deepen, and faith becomes something people actually experience, not just talk about. That kind of legacy matters.

A strong, relational culture doesn't stay confined to Sunday mornings or church buildings. When people feel deeply connected and cared for, they start carrying that same love into the places they live, work, and gather. It begins to shape neighborhoods, classrooms, and offices. People notice. They may not always know what it is, but they can feel the difference. That kind of love makes an impact far beyond the church walls.

The culture we build influences how we live out our faith every day. It creates the kind of environment where courage, kindness, and compassion can take root and grow. As we commit to this kind of culture, we find ourselves more equipped and more inspired to share the hope we've found. And over time, this way of living brings people together and draws them closer to the heart of Christ, inviting invites them into His mission.

# Chapter 10
# Community Beyond the Four Walls

## Beyond the Walls

The gospel was never meant to stay tucked away inside a building or reserved for Sunday mornings. It's not something we pick up when we walk through the church doors and leave behind when we step out. The gospel is alive, meant to move, breathe, and flow into every part of our lives. Unfortunately, too often, we box it in. We treat our faith like it belongs in a separate, safe space, a place where we worship, pray, and feel inspired but don't always let that same fire spill over into our homes, schools, workplaces, or neighborhoods.

The gospel was always meant to go beyond the walls of the church. It's not a private treasure; it's a call to action. It's about showing up in the everyday moments and letting God's love come alive in practical, tangible ways. It's about loving so deeply, so authentically, that it doesn't just change us; it changes the world around us. This final chapter is an invitation to break down those walls and take the gospel out where it belongs—in the messiness of real life, where love can truly transform lives and communities.

One of the biggest reasons we hesitate to take the gospel beyond church walls is fear. Fear of rejection, fear of being judged, or even fear of saying the wrong thing can stop us in our tracks. It's easy to think, *"I'm not good at this,"* or *"Someone else would do a better job sharing their faith."* But the truth is that God doesn't expect us to be perfect; He just asks us to be willing. 2 Timothy 1:7 reminds us, *"For the Spirit God gave us does not make us timid, but gives us power, love, and self-discipline."* God gives us everything we need to step out, even when we feel unprepared or unsure.

Another reason we hold back is staying in our comfort zones. It's so tempting to stay in the familiar, where faith feels safe and routine. Let's face it, sharing the gospel can feel intimidating or inconvenient. Life gets busy, and it's easy to think, *"I'm doing enough just by going to church and trying to be a good person."* But when we stay comfortable, we miss out on the incredible joy that comes from stepping out in faith. The early church didn't let comfort define them. They took risks, met people where they were, and shared the love of Jesus with boldness because they knew this message was too important to keep to themselves.

Then there's the uncertainty. Maybe you've wondered, *"How do I even bring this up?"* or *"What if someone asks me a question I can't answer?"* But here's the thing, sharing the gospel is not about delivering the perfect speech, it's about building relationships and letting people see Jesus in how you live. Sometimes, the most powerful way to share your faith isn't with words but through simple acts of kindness like a meal for a neighbor who's struggling, a listening ear for a friend who's hurting, or a small gesture that reminds someone they're not alone. Those small actions can speak louder than any preaching.

To move past these barriers, we need to change how we think. We don't have to wait for the perfect moment or making sure we have everything figured out. It really comes down to simply showing up. It's about asking, *"Who can I encourage today? Where can I be a light right now?"* When we take even the smallest steps to reflect God's love, something incredible happens. Not only do we impact others, but our faith grows deeper, too. It's a chain reaction of love that starts with one simple act of obedience.

Through the early church we see a powerful picture of what it means to live out this kind of love. A community that was deeply connected. They were connected by their belief but also by the way they lived their lives together. These believers devoted themselves to teaching, fellowship, breaking bread, and prayer. They didn't treat faith as something they kept private or compartmentalized. Instead, they shared their lives, their homes, and even their resources. It's a noticeable shift from what many people are used to in church today, where real connection can feel rare instead of normal.

What stands out about them is how intentional they were about relationships. They gathered in formal settings, they met regularly in homes, and shared meals while building deep connections. They were unified, described as being *"of one heart and soul"* (Acts 4:32). It might feel like a bit of a cliché, but they truly lived as a family.

Their love for one another wasn't surface level. They practiced radical generosity, selling property and possessions to make sure no one was in need. This kind of selfless care wasn't about fulfilling obligations or looking good; it was about genuinely loving their neighbors as themselves (Matthew 22:39).

Imagine what this kind of community could look like today. A place where no one feels alone or forgotten, where needs are met, and where relationships go beyond polite conversations on Sunday mornings. This is what happens when love moves beyond walls, it creates a family that transforms the world around it.

Paul's words in 1 Corinthians 13 remind us that love is meant to be at the center of everything we do as followers of Jesus. No matter how impressive or sacrificial our actions may seem, they lose their meaning if love isn't behind them. And this love isn't meant to stay quiet or hidden. It moves us. It shows up in how we treat people, how we respond when someone is hurting, and how we create space for others to feel seen, valued, and supported.

So, what does this love look like when it moves beyond good intentions? How do we take it out into the world, letting it breathe life into our families, communities, and even strangers we encounter? This is a call to step out of the familiar and the comfortable. It's a challenge to live boldly, love audaciously, and let the gospel ripple far beyond ourselves.

Faith comes to life through the choices we make and the way we care for others. It moves beyond words and shows up in our actions, shaping how we treat people and how we respond to the needs around us. When love becomes our starting point, it naturally leaves an impact that others can't ignore.

## The Essential Ingredient

In 1 Corinthians 13:1-3, Paul paints a vivid and challenging picture of what happens when love is missing from our lives and actions. He writes, "If I speak in the tongues of men or of angels, but do not have love, I am only a resounding gong or a clanging cymbal." In other words, no matter how eloquent, spiritual, or sacrificial we appear, it all amounts to nothing without love. Paul is crystal clear: love is the essential core of everything we do. Without it, even the most remarkable actions lose their meaning.

Loneliness is one of the most significant challenges facing our world today. It's this overwhelming feeling of being unseen, unheard, and disconnected, even in a crowd. Psychologist Dr. John Cacioppo, one of the leading researchers on loneliness, described it as a "biological warning system" signaling that we need connection, much like hunger signals a need for food. His studies revealed that chronic loneliness can actually be physically harmful, leading to increased stress, weakened immune systems, and even higher risks of heart disease.

The beautiful thing about love is how it can shift everything. Real, intentional care has a way of reaching people right where they are. It reminds them they matter. In a church community, it doesn't take much to make that kind of impact. A genuine smile, a meaningful conversation, or simply inviting someone out for coffee can leave a lasting impression. These simple moments can create the kind of connection people are quietly hoping for, especially in a world that can feel distant and divided.

It begins with small, everyday moments. A kind word, a thoughtful gesture, a little extra time spent really listening. These simple acts go further than we think. When someone feels genuinely loved, they tend to pass that love along. It spreads. And when a church leans into that kind of care, people around them start to notice. It shows the gospel in a way that feels real; through hope, healing, and the kind of connection that sticks with you.

In the church at Corinth, Paul had to step in because some believers started using their spiritual gifts to boost their own image. Speaking in tongues or prophesying became more about showing off than serving others. This mindset created tension in the church and left people feeling divided, envious, and unsure of their place. Paul brought clarity by reminding them of what really matters. The value of a gift isn't found in how impressive it looks but in the love that fuels it. Without love, even the most powerful gifts lose their impact. Henri Nouwen put it beautifully in *Life of the Beloved* when he wrote, "Our lives are unique stones in the mosaic of human existence—priceless and irreplaceable." Love is what holds those pieces together, forming something meaningful and lasting.

Acts 2:44–45 paints a powerful picture of love in action. The early believers lived with open hands and open hearts. They sold their belongings and shared with anyone in need, not because they were trying to impress anyone, but because they genuinely cared. Their generosity made Jesus's words in John 13 come alive: *"Love one another. As I have loved you, so you must love one another. By this everyone will know that you are my disciples, if you love one another."*

This kind of love wasn't transactional or surface-level. It was real. It built a community where people felt truly seen and supported. That love didn't stop with them either. It overflowed. The way they cared for one another reflected something much bigger, it showed the world what God's love actually looks like when it's lived out.

Think about how different things could be if we started loving like that today. What would happen if our churches became places where everyone's needs were met because we were willing to share what we had? Imagine the shift if we stopped measuring people by their skills or roles and started seeing them through the eyes of Christ. Henri Nouwen said it best in *Life of the Beloved*: "Being the beloved expresses the core truth of our existence." The early church lived that out in practical ways. They made sure people experienced love in tangible ways—through genuine care and consistent, everyday actions.

Paul's teaching pushes us to dig deeper and reflect on our own motivations. We need to ask ourselves tough questions: Why am I serving? Is it because I genuinely care for the people around me, or is it because I want to be noticed or appreciated? Am I using the talents and gifts God has given me to build others up, or am I using them to boost my own ego? These aren't easy questions, but they're necessary if we're serious about living out our faith.

Love is what gives our actions real weight. Without it, even the biggest gestures can feel empty. It's like handing someone a beautifully wrapped gift, only for them to open it and find nothing inside. The outside might look great, but without anything real at the center, it leaves them feeling let down. That's what happens when love isn't behind what we do, it loses its impact and doesn't leave the mark we hoped it would.

Paul's message is clear. Love transforms everything it touches. It turns simple moments into something meaningful and powerful. A quiet meal shared with a neighbor can carry more weight than a public act meant to impress. Love brings depth to our service and makes it a reflection of God's heart. Without it, even the best intentions fall flat and miss the opportunity to truly reveal who He is.

When love is at the center of what we do, our actions begin to reflect something much bigger than us. They show glimpses of God's kindness, His grace, and the compassion He freely gives. But when we're driven by pride or selfishness, the focus shifts away from God and lands on us. That's why Paul is so clear about the importance of love. It's what gives our actions lasting impact. It's what helps people see who God really is through the way we live and serve.

## Faith in Action: Love That Moves

Paul's emphasis on love lines up with the direct challenge James gives in James 2:15–17: "If one of you says to [a brother or sister], 'Go in peace; keep warm and well fed,' but does nothing about their physical needs, what good is it?" James doesn't hold back. He calls out the disconnect between words and action. It's the kind of question that makes us pause and take a closer look at whether our faith is really showing up in the way we live. Both Paul and James point to the same truth that faith and love were always meant to move us toward action. Real faith isn't passive. It steps in, shows up, and does something about the needs in front of us.

This is something believers have lived out for generations. Teresa of Ávila, a 16th-century mystic and reformer, once wrote, "Christ has no body now on earth but yours, no hands but yours, no feet but yours. Yours are the eyes through which Christ's compassion must look out on the world. Yours are the feet with which He is to go about doing good; yours are the hands with which He is to bless His people." Her words are a powerful reminder that faith is meant to be lived, not just discussed. God's love reaches others through what we do, how we serve, and the way we show up in everyday moments.

Paul and James both call us to take our faith seriously by putting love into action. Paul reminds us that love gives meaning to everything we do. James brings it even closer to home by showing how empty love feels when it's not backed up by action. Imagine telling someone who's hungry, "Hope you find something to eat," and then walking away. The words might sound kind, but without any follow-through, they don't mean much. Both of these voices are pushing us to close the gap between what we believe and how we live. Love fuels what we do, and our actions show whether that love is real.

> Love fuels what we do, and our actions show whether that love is real.

One of the challenges many churches face today is putting too much focus on programs and not enough on people. Programs can serve a purpose. They bring structure, help organize ministry, and open doors for involvement. But when programs start to matter more than the relationships they're supposed to support, something gets lost. Instead of building strong, meaningful connections, we risk turning discipleship into a checklist of attendance and participation.

The early church looked very different from that. Their focus wasn't on managing events or tracking growth. It was on being present with one another and caring for each other's needs. They built community through love, not schedules. Discipleship happened naturally over shared meals, in honest conversations, and through simple, consistent acts of care and service. It was personal, grounded, and deeply relational.

James K.A. Smith, in *You Are What You Love*, highlights this shift in focus: *"Our actions, habits, and practices shape our hearts and desires."* Programs, when detached from relationships, often fail to cultivate these lasting habits. On the other hand, relational discipleship creates space for hearts to be shaped and lives to be transformed.

Programs can be helpful when they're used the right way. They're meant to be tools that support the bigger purpose of discipleship. The real goal is investing in people, walking with them, sharing life, and helping one another grow in Christ. When programs create space for that kind of connection, they can make a big impact. But if they take the place of real relationships, we lose sight of what the gospel is really calling us to do.

In a world filled with quick fixes and shallow gestures, real love that actually shows up and gives of itself catches people's attention. It points them to something deeper. That kind of love becomes a light that leads others toward Christ. When love and action work together, something powerful takes place. Our lives start to reflect the gospel in ways that go beyond words.

## The Quiet Legacy of Tabitha

We don't talk about it often, but a lot of what passes for humility today is really self-promotion in disguise. People say they're serving God or helping others, but deep down, they're building a platform. They want to be noticed. They want their name attached to whatever good is happening. Even in the church, it's easy to slip into the mindset that visibility equals value. Somewhere along the way, we've started measuring impact by likes, influence, or how many people are watching. The truth is that you don't have to be famous to be effective. You just have to be faithful with what God has placed in your hands.

But there's a story in Scripture that challenges that mindset, one that doesn't get talked about much. It only appears once, and the woman at the center of it is never mentioned again, yet her life left a mark that's hard to forget.

The story of Tabitha, also known as Dorcas, in Acts 9:36–42, gives us a beautiful picture of what faith and love look like when they're lived out in everyday life. She lived in the busy port city of Joppa and quietly committed herself to helping those in need, especially widows and the poor. Her story only takes up a few verses, but the impact she made was powerful. Tabitha wasn't looking for recognition or trying to make a name for herself. She simply cared and her life reflected that care in ways that still speak to us today.

Tabitha's life brings Micah 6:8 to mind: *"He has shown you, O mortal, what is good. And what does the Lord require of you? To act justly and to love mercy and to walk humbly with your God."* Her love showed up in practical ways. It wasn't loud or showy, but it was constant and sincere. She made clothes for those who couldn't afford them. She cared for widows who were often overlooked. Her hands and her heart were always at work, meeting real needs with quiet faithfulness.

Tabitha's story reminds us how powerful small acts of love can be. She wasn't a preacher, and she didn't stand in front of crowds, but she used what she had. Her skills, her time, and her compassion were all offered freely. When she passed away, the impact she had made was unmistakable. The widows she had cared for stood together, holding the garments she had made for them. Each piece of clothing told a story. Through their tears, they remembered her kindness. Their grief spoke volumes, but so did their love for her.

In moments like that, it becomes clear that what we do for others truly matters. Tabitha didn't make headlines, but she left behind something lasting. Her story shows that when we choose to love in small, consistent ways, we build something that goes far beyond ourselves. These simple acts become the thread that holds a community together. Even when the world doesn't take notice, God sees it all. And what we place in His hands becomes part of something far greater than we could ever create on our own.

Tabitha's life shows us what "quiet love" really looks like. It doesn't seek applause or recognition. It simply gives. And that kind of love reaches further than we imagine. So if you've ever questioned whether your everyday efforts matter, let Tabitha's story be the reminder. They absolutely do. Every moment of kindness carries eternal weight when it comes from a heart aligned with God.

Her story continues to speak because it reflects something so needed in the world today. She didn't try to stand out. She chose to care, and in doing that, she made a difference that still inspires us. We often hear about people who do big things, but Tabitha's life reminds us that consistent, faithful love changes lives too. We don't need a spotlight to make an impact. We just need to be present and willing to serve.

In today's world, individualism gets a lot of attention. We're encouraged to chase our goals, protect our time, and focus on our own success. But there's a cost to that. Relationships can suffer when everything becomes centered on personal gain. Sadly, if we allow that mindset to creep into the church, it will make community feel shallow and disconnected. When that happens, faith becomes something we manage on our own instead of something we share.

The early church paints a different picture. They lived with a sense of shared purpose. Galatians 6:2 says, "Carry each other's burdens," and that's exactly what they did. They built a community where everyone had something to give and no one was left behind. They didn't compete or compare. They cared. Their strength came from walking together, side by side.

Tabitha lived out that same spirit. She wasn't focused on herself. She gave her time and energy to lift others up, especially those who were often forgotten. Her legacy was found in the lives she touched, not in titles or accomplishments. She showed us what it looks like to move from "me" to "we." Her story paints a clear picture of what happens when we build a community grounded in compassion.

This shift is just as important for the church today. When we embrace the truth that we belong to each other, we begin to reflect God's heart for unity. Romans 12:10 encourages us to "be devoted to one another in love. Honor one another above yourselves." When this becomes the way we live, the church becomes a place of healing, support, and growth. One act of love at a time, the community is strengthened, and lives are transformed.

## Live Like Jesus

At the center of the gospel is a love so deep and personal that it has the power to change everything. John 3:16 puts it plainly: "For God so loved the world that He gave His one and only Son." That kind of love goes beyond a comforting idea or a story we keep at a distance. It's real, active, and intentional. Through the way He lived and the way He gave His life, Jesus showed us what love in motion really looks like. A love that gives, that forgives, and that meets people exactly where they are.

Dr. Martin Luther King Jr. once said, "Love is the only force capable of transforming an enemy into a friend." That captures the kind of love Jesus invites us to live out. This love doesn't have to be loud or dramatic to be powerful. It shows up in small, consistent ways. Moments that may feel simple, but they carry the kind of love that heals, restores, and brings people together.

Paul reminds us in Ephesians 2:10 that we were "created in Christ Jesus to do good works, which God prepared in advance for us to do." Loving like Jesus means choosing to step into that purpose. It means paying attention to the people around us, offering forgiveness when it's tough, and standing up for those who are often overlooked. It's lived out in everyday interactions—in the way we speak, the way we listen, and the way we carry God's heart into whatever space we're in.

Love doesn't sit still. It moves, it takes action, and it makes itself known. Whether that looks like serving at a local shelter, encouraging someone who feels like giving up, or simply sitting beside a friend in silence, love is something we do. And at the core of it is presence. Loving like Jesus means being there, even when it's uncomfortable or inconvenient. Sometimes showing up is the most powerful way to let someone know they matter. That kind of presence says, "You're seen. You're loved. You're not alone."

Love also plays a role in the choices we make every single day. Whether you're at work, in class, at home, or running errands, there's always an opportunity to reflect God's love. You can pause in the middle of a busy moment and ask, "How can I show love here?" Sometimes it's choosing patience instead of frustration. Other times it's responding with kindness when someone is difficult, or giving generously when someone is in need. When love becomes the filter for our decisions, the way we live starts to shift, and people notice.

What's beautiful about this way of living is that it doesn't require a spotlight. You don't need a platform or a microphone to make a difference. The love we show in everyday moments often speaks louder than any message we could preach. When someone sees a consistent, selfless kind of love that sticks around and shows up, they begin to wonder what's behind it. And that question opens the door to the answer, Jesus.

> *You don't need a platform or a microphone to make a difference.*

Living this way won't always feel easy, but it's what we're invited into. It changes us, and it changes the people around us. So let's lean into that calling.

Let's choose to live like Jesus—by loving with courage, serving with consistency, and showing the world what the gospel looks like when it becomes a way of life.

## A Community Transformed

If we don't allow our communities to be shaped by God's love, we risk becoming everything people are already skeptical about. We turn into groups that feel more like clubs than families. People slip through the cracks. Needs go unnoticed. And church becomes another place where people feel unseen and unheard. Honestly, this is why so many today hesitate to walk through church doors. They've experienced surface-level connection or felt like outsiders in places that were supposed to feel like home.

But when we embrace the kind of love that Jesus modeled, something shifts.

The early church gives us a clear picture of what happens when love turns into action. In Acts 2, we see a group of believers who not only talked about love but they lived it out in their daily lives. They shared what they had, took care of each other's needs, and made sure no one was left behind. Their love wasn't something they used to impress others. It was honest, sacrificial, and deeply personal. And it made a difference. People on the outside could see something real was happening. The community was so compelling that others wanted to be part of it. Scripture says, "The Lord added to their number daily those who were being saved" (Acts 2:47).

Jean Vanier, the founder of the L'Arche communities, once said, "Love doesn't mean doing extraordinary or heroic things. It means knowing how to do ordinary things with tenderness." That captures the heart of what made the early church so powerful. They weren't chasing attention or trying to create impressive moments.

They simply loved well. Their kindness and generosity created space for people to feel safe, valued, and drawn toward Jesus.

Now think about what could happen if we loved like that today. It doesn't take anything huge or dramatic. It starts with showing up and paying attention to the people around us. Maybe it's meeting a need quietly, without asking for credit. Maybe it's choosing to listen, to give, or to care when no one else does. These simple moments can carry a kind of love that sticks with people. When love is lived out instead of only spoken about, it begins to leave a mark. It shapes hearts, influences lives, and moves throughout entire communities. And that kind of love still speaks just as powerfully today as it did back then.

## Breaking the Walls, Building the Kingdom

The gospel was never meant to stay quiet or contained. It was always meant to move. It calls us to step outside our comfort zones and into the lives of others, shining light where it's needed most and bringing hope to those who are hurting. The early church understood this. Their love wasn't passive. It showed up boldly and changed lives.

Living out the gospel starts with everyday decisions. It looks like pausing to listen when someone really needs to talk. It means choosing forgiveness when it would be easier to walk away. It's giving generously, not just with money but with your time, your presence, and your care. Tabitha's story is such a powerful reminder of what this looks like. Her quiet, consistent love made such an impact that when she died, her community couldn't imagine life without her. The clothes she made and the compassion she gave became reminders of a life poured out in service. And through her legacy, God moved in a miraculous way and gave her life back.

Love like that doesn't need a spotlight. It makes others feel known and valued. That's the kind of love that reflects who Jesus is—the one who came to serve, not to be served. And when we love like He did, people get to see what the gospel really looks like.

So here's where the challenge hits home. What are we doing with what we've received? Are we willing to carry it into a world that's desperate for something real? The gospel comes alive when it moves through us. It starts with building relationships and showing up in the places that aren't always easy. That's where the real work of love happens.

This is what "community beyond the four walls" is all about. It's about being present where it counts most, right in the middle of people's lives. It means loving in a way that costs us something, because that's the example Jesus gave us. And when we let that love shape our words, our choices, and our rhythms, it begins to spill out into the world around us. That's when things begin to change.

So here's the question: are you ready to take that step? Are you willing to let your faith move beyond comfort and into action? This is the moment to lean in. Let's take the love of Jesus with us into the streets, into homes, into schools and workplaces. Let's carry it with grace, with courage, and with open hands. Because this is how the gospel becomes visible. This is how it touches hearts. This is how it changes lives.

# Conclusion

## Living the Relational Church

When we look back at the early church, we see a group of people who were deeply connected. They shared a clear sense of purpose, and their love for one another was hard to miss. Their faith wasn't something they saved for weekends or kept inside the walls of a synagogue. It was woven into their daily lives. It shaped how they learned, how they prayed, how they ate together, and how they met each other's needs. They lived with generosity and compassion, making sure no one was left behind. What set them apart wasn't perfection, it was the way they stayed devoted to each other and to the mission they shared. The way they loved made people curious. It made people want to be part of it. That kind of community speaks louder than any sermon.

In today's church, it can be easy to lose sight of that. We often put our trust in systems and structures, thinking they'll carry the weight of what only relationships were meant to hold. Programs can help, but they were never meant to replace people. At the core, the church is not a logo or a location. It's a family. A group of people brought together by the love of Jesus, called to grow together and reach the world with that same love. When we begin to shift our focus back to that—to relationships that are honest, intentional, and Spirit-led—we begin to see what the church was always meant to be. And that shift has the power to bring life back into our communities in ways that no strategy ever could.

## Returning to Relational Roots

The early church reminds us that relationships are where real discipleship begins. They weren't focused on numbers or how polished their gatherings looked. What mattered most was how deeply they knew and cared for each other. Their way of doing life together created space for real spiritual growth. They shared meals. They carried each other's burdens. They encouraged one another to keep going, even when things were hard. And through those relationships, faith took root and grew.

At the core of relational discipleship is the decision to keep showing up with love in the ordinary moments. It doesn't have to be big or impressive. It just has to be real. Sometimes it looks like a simple conversation over coffee. Other times it's taking a few minutes to pray with someone who's feeling overwhelmed, or dropping off a meal when a friend needs support. These moments may seem small, but they have a way of creating connection and sparking change. When we live like this, with love at the center, we build the kind of community that makes people feel like they belong. And that's where transformation begins.

## A Call to Mutual Care

The gospel invites us to move beyond living for ourselves and start leaning into each other. It calls us to a deeper kind of care, a life where we show up for one another with real love and real commitment.

When Paul wrote, "Be devoted to one another in love," he wasn't describing something casual. He was pointing to a way of life where no one is left to carry their burdens alone. The early believers lived this out beautifully. They made sure everyone was cared for, and they didn't hold back when it came to generosity or compassion.

That same calling still stands today. We're invited to live with open hands and open hearts, sharing our resources, offering our attention, and showing up with genuine presence. Mutual care doesn't come from doing something dramatic. It grows from a steady commitment to see people the way God sees them; valuable, loved, and worthy of our investment. Every time we choose to love like that, we're building something that lasts. We're creating a legacy that mirrors God's heart and draws others closer to Him.

## The Spirit-Led Community

The early church wasn't fueled by clever strategies or polished plans. They depended on the Holy Spirit. They prayed together, listened for God's direction, and moved forward in obedience. They trusted that God would lead their relationships, their mission, and their growth. And what happened as a result was beautiful. People from different cultures, backgrounds, and economic situations came together in ways that didn't make sense by human standards. Their unity wasn't forced. It was formed through the power of God working in surrendered hearts.

That same kind of unity is still possible today, but it doesn't come from trying to control or manufacture it. It comes when we surrender to the Spirit and allow God to lead. When we walk with Him, we begin to see the beauty of diversity rather than division. Ephesians 4:3–6 calls us to "maintain the unity of the Spirit through the bond of peace," reminding us that we are already united in Christ. Our job is to protect that unity by staying rooted in love, humility, and grace. When we do, the world gets to see what it looks like when God's people live in step with His Spirit.

## A Challenge to Live Out the Gospel

So here we are, at the end of this journey, but in many ways, it's only the beginning. Everything we've explored comes down to one central question: what does it really mean to live as the church? Not the building. Not the programs. But the people. The real, relational, sometimes messy, beautifully imperfect people who are connected to God and committed to each other. That's where the gospel leads us. Not to performance or religious routine, but into something more honest, something that reaches the heart.

> We are being invited to become the kind of church that values people more than performance

Relational discipleship is a way of life. It's walking with Jesus in a way that shapes who you are while walking with others at the same time. It's choosing to grow together, even when it's inconvenient or uncomfortable. The early followers of Jesus showed us what this looked like. They were known for their love, their consistency, and their deep dependence on the Spirit of God.

That same call is still in front of us. We are being invited to become the kind of church that values people more than performance, where relationships carry more weight than routines. Earlier in the journey, we reflected on the truth that the most important thing in life is not what we do but who we are becoming. That reminder still holds strong. Living this way doesn't mean adding more to our schedule. It means allowing the love of God to shape us from within. It means choosing a different pace and a different posture, one that reflects the heart of Jesus.

Throughout this book, we've talked about what that life looks like. It's choosing to see discipleship as a shared experience, not a one-time event or a set of classes. It's building environments where people feel safe to open up and know they'll be supported. It's trusting the Holy Spirit more than our plans. And it's leaning into relationships that will outlast us and ripple into the future with love and faith.

Let's be honest though, this way of living won't happen on its own. It requires intentionality. It asks us to tear down the walls that keep us distant. It invites us to stop asking what we can get and start asking how we can give. Every interaction becomes a moment where we reflect the love of Jesus.

This is the heart of a relational church. It isn't driven by numbers or polished presentations. It is driven by real, consistent, transformative love. It's personal. It goes beyond the surface. It reaches people where they are and lets them know they belong. And when that kind of love shows up, people begin to see Jesus for who He truly is.

So now the question is in front of you. Are you ready to step into this kind of life? Are you willing to release the habits of transactional faith and take hold of something more meaningful? Because when the gospel moves through you, it won't stop with you. It will impact every person you encounter.

This isn't something to admire from a distance. It's something to live out. The gospel was never meant to stay tucked inside church walls or hidden in our private moments with God. It's meant to go with you. Into your relationships. Into your daily conversations. People are searching for a kind of faith that feels genuine. They want to see if the church really can be a place that looks like home.

This is your moment. Be bold. Build a community that carries God's love with strength and sincerity. Show the people around you what it looks like to follow Jesus—not with perfection, but with authenticity and grace. Because this life of faith is meant to be close, personal, and filled with the kind of love that truly changes everything.

## Living the Relational Church: Your Next Step

So, what's next? Everything we've explored in this book points to one thing: you have a role to play. Whether you're leading from the front, walking faithfully as part of your church family, or searching for a place to call home, this isn't just theory, it's a way of life. The relational church is built one connection at a time, and it begins with you.

### If You're a Leader

You hold the keys to culture. The way you lead, speak, and engage sets the tone for everything else. You have the power to create an environment where relationships come first. This is the space where people feel truly seen, known, and valued.

Here's where to start:

- Take a moment to reflect. Are there areas where relationships have taken a back seat to tasks or results? What small changes could you make to prioritize people?

- Lead by example. Show your team what it looks like to listen well, to encourage consistently, and to build trust through everyday actions.
- Start with one change. It could be as simple as spending more time connecting with your staff or fostering intentional moments of prayer and encouragement.

Relational leadership grows when we choose presence over pressure. When you lead with love, you set the foundation for a culture that lasts.

## If You're a Church Member

You might think the responsibility for creating a relational church rest solely on leaders, but here's the truth: it's all of us. You have just as much influence in shaping the culture of your church as anyone else.

So, what can you do?

- Step in. Look for ways to connect with others. Invite someone for coffee or simply be the person who smiles and says hello.
- Support your leaders. They need your encouragement, your prayers, and your partnership. Let them know you're with them.
- Be the change you want to see. Show kindness, practice empathy, and live out the relational values you hope to see more of in your church.

The church functions best when it reflects the closeness and care of a family. Strength comes when everyone leans in, brings what they have, and supports one another along the way.

## If You're a Disillusioned Christian

First, let me say this: I'm so sorry for the pain you've experienced. Whether it's hurt, disappointment, or feeling unseen, your story matters. You matter. And even though it may not feel like it right now, there's still hope.

Here's what I want you to know:

- Take your time. Healing doesn't happen overnight, and it's okay to go slow. God's not in a rush, and neither should you be.
- Use what you've learned. Plant yourself in a church where relationships are real, where people are known and cared for, and where the focus stays on spiritual growth and genuine connection.
- Keep your heart open. Trusting again can feel risky, but the right community—the kind God has for you—will be worth it.

There is a place for you, a church where you can belong and thrive. Don't let past hurt keep you from the healing that's waiting for you.

## Where do We Go from Here?

No matter your background or where your journey has taken you, the invitation is the same. Let's build something meaningful together. A relational church becomes real through small, everyday choices that reflect love and intention. When we show up with purpose, ready to serve, willing to listen, and open to connection, God meets us there. And when He is in the middle of it, things begin to shift.

Leading with love and staying rooted in relationships has the power to transform everything around you. It influences your personal walk with Christ. It shapes the culture of your church. And it extends far into the community beyond its walls. When the gospel flows through our relationships, it leaves behind healing, hope, and lasting impact.

You don't need to have it all figured out. What matters most is showing up with a heart that is willing, open, and surrendered. Change begins in those places. Through honest conversations, simple acts of kindness, and consistent faithfulness, something meaningful starts to grow.

Real impact grows where love is sincere. It shows up where people feel welcomed, seen, and cared for. It is in those environments where God's presence becomes undeniable, not because of how perfect things look, but because of how deeply people are loved.

This is how we reflect God's heart to the world. This is how the gospel comes to life.

When the church leans into what is personal and real, it becomes powerful.

Powerful enough to change the world.

# Epilogue
# A Vision for the Future

What if we actually lived this?

What if the Church, across the street and across the world, paused long enough to breathe, look around, and say, "This is personal"?

What if this wasn't only a powerful message or a meaningful conversation, but the heartbeat behind the way we lead, love, and live each day?

Picture a church where people come through the doors and immediately feel seen. A place where no one goes unnoticed because connection is more important than a task, and people matter more than polished plans. Imagine stepping into a room that feels like home, not because of the furniture or the lights, but because the people are present. A place where you're welcomed without a title and embraced without needing to earn it.

What would happen if our conversations became more important than our platforms? What if our planning meetings opened with prayer and honest check-ins because we cared just as much about someone's soul as we did about the Sunday schedule?

I believe we'd begin to see something sacred take shape. Pastors would breathe easier, not because their responsibilities changed, but because they're no longer carrying them alone. Volunteers would serve with joy, not out of duty, but because they feel connected to a bigger purpose. Families would begin to heal. Generations would start listening to each other again. Communities would shift, not because of clever ideas, but because of faithful, Spirit-led relationships.

I believe young people would stay, not for entertainment, but because they see something real. I believe skeptics would feel safe enough to speak honestly. Wanderers would return, not to a system, but to a Savior they can recognize through the way His people love.

This is what happens when we choose authenticity over image. When ministry stops being a list of tasks and becomes a way of living that reflects the heart of Jesus.

The world isn't looking for something more polished. It's longing for people who will slow down, cry with those who are grieving, celebrate with those who are rejoicing, and notice the one who feels invisible.

And the beautiful part is, you don't need a big building or a massive budget to do this. All it takes is a willing heart that says, "I'm here. I care. Let's walk this together."

As we move forward, may this message stay with you. Not as an idea to admire, but as a life to live. Be part of building a church that feels like family. Create spaces where love is more than a word—it's the way we move through the world.

In the end, it's not business—it's personal.

# Sources & Biblical References

## PREFACE

**Supporting Biblical References:**

1. Isaiah 55:8–9 – This passage highlights the difference between God's relational ways and the world's transactional mindset, serving as the foundation for the message of this chapter.

## INTRODUCTION

**Books Referenced:**

1. James K.A. Smith, Desiring the Kingdom (Baker Academic, 2009)

2. Quoted to illustrate how consumer culture can influence the way we experience worship, shifting our identity from participants in covenantal relationships to consumers of religious content.

**Supporting Biblical References:**

1. James 1:27 – Defines pure religion as caring for the vulnerable and staying unstained by the world, setting a foundation for relational ministry.

2. Acts 2:42–47 – Shows the early church's model of fellowship, generosity, shared life, and community rooted in faith.

3. John 13:34–35 – Jesus calls His disciples to love one another as the primary evidence of belonging to Him.

## CHAPTER 1 – THE FOUNDATION OF A RELATIONAL CHURCH

**Books Referenced:**

1. C.S. Lewis, *The Four Loves* (HarperCollins, 1960)

    o  Quoted to highlight the power of shared experience and vulnerability in the formation of true friendship and connection.

2. Julianne Holt-Lunstad, "Social Relationships and Mortality Risk: A Meta-analytic Review," *PLOS Medicine*, 2010

    o  Cited for data linking weak social relationships to higher mortality risk, emphasizing the urgent need for meaningful connection.

3. Christine Pohl, *Living into Community* (Eerdmans, 2012)

    o  Referenced for her practical insights on truth-telling and gratitude as foundations for healthy and lasting community life.

4. N.T. Wright, *Simply Christian* (HarperOne, 2006)

    o   Quoted to describe the church as a community of love that reflects the kind of life God desires for us.

5. Timothy Keller, *The Meaning of Marriage* (Penguin Books, 2011)

    o   Cited to define Christian love as sacrificial, unconditional, and focused on the good of others.

6. Francis Chan, *Crazy Love* (David C. Cook, 2008)

    o   Quoted to reinforce that we are most alive when we love and give actively, which aligns with the purpose of a relational church.

## Supporting Biblical References:

1. Matthew 18:21-22 – Jesus' teaching on forgiveness, encouraging persistent grace in community.

2. John 13:35 – Jesus identifies love as the defining trait of His disciples.

3. Luke 19:5 – Jesus' personal invitation to Zacchaeus shows the importance of intentional connection.

4. Mark 12:30-31 – The two greatest commandments that call us to love God and others deeply.

5. Hebrews 13:1-2, 16 – A clear charge to love, show hospitality, and share with others as acts that please God.

6. John 17:22 – Jesus' prayer for unity, reflecting God's heart for deep connection among believers.

7. James 1:27 – Defines true religion as caring for the vulnerable, emphasizing practical love.

8. Acts 2:42–47 – Shows the early church's model of unity, generosity, and shared spiritual life.

## CHAPTER 2 - BEYOND PERFORMANCE AND RITUALS

### Books Referenced:

1. A.W. Tozer, *The Pursuit of God* (Christian Publications, 1948)

    o Quoted to emphasize the danger of mistaking ministry activity for intimacy with God's presence.

2. John Piper, *Desiring God* (Multnomah, 1986)

    o Quoted to underscore the truth that God is most glorified when we find true satisfaction in Him alone.

3. Timothy Keller, *The Meaning of Marriage* (Dutton, 2011)

    o Quoted to describe the Christian view of love as sacrificial, unconditional, and centered on the other.

4. Francis Chan, *Crazy Love* (David C Cook, 2008)

    o Quoted to affirm that we are most alive when we actively love and give of ourselves.

5. N.T. Wright, *Simply Christian* (HarperOne, 2006)

    o Quoted to cast a vision of Christian community as a reflection of God's intention for human flourishing.

## Supporting Biblical References:

1. 1 Samuel 3:7 – Reveals that knowing God intimately goes beyond serving Him in proximity or tradition.

2. Matthew 7:22–23 – Jesus warns about the danger of outward religious performance disconnected from genuine relationship.

3. Matthew 6:1 – A caution against practicing righteousness for show, encouraging personal devotion over public recognition.

4. Luke 1:34 – Highlights the biblical meaning of "know" as deep intimacy, providing context for our relationship with God.

5. Isaiah 58 – A rebuke of empty rituals, calling believers to genuine love, justice, and mercy.

6. Matthew 28:19 – The Great Commission, framed not only as preaching but embodying God's love in daily life.

# CHAPTER 3 - MOVING BEYOND SELF-CENTEREDNESS

## Books Referenced:

1. C.S. Lewis, *Mere Christianity* (HarperOne, 2001)

    o Quoted to illustrate how choosing to love—especially when we don't feel like it—leads to authentic love and deeper connection.

2. Brennan Manning, *The Ragamuffin Gospel* (Multnomah, 2005)

- Cited to highlight the disconnect between outward religious expression and genuine Christian living, and the impact that has on unbelievers.

3. Barna Group Research, 2022

    - Mentioned for data showing that faith based solely on religious activity often leads to less satisfaction and higher anxiety than authentic relational faith.

## Supporting Biblical References:

1. Revelation 2:4 – Jesus rebukes the Ephesian church for abandoning their first love, showing that works without love miss the heart of the gospel.

2. Philippians 2:3-4 – A call to humility, urging believers to put the needs of others above their own.

3. Matthew 23:11 – Jesus teaches that true greatness is found in serving others, not in pursuing recognition.

4. John 13:34-35 – Jesus commands His followers to love as He loved, establishing love as the defining mark of discipleship.

5. Romans 12:2 – A reminder to resist cultural conformity and pursue transformation through God's values.

6. John 21:15-19 – Jesus restores Peter after his failure, showing grace and calling him back to love-driven purpose.

7. Acts 2:42-47 – Describes the relational nature of the early church, highlighting generosity, fellowship, and shared spiritual life.

# CHAPTER 4 - THE MINISTRY OF PRESENCE

## Books Referenced:

1. N.T. Wright, *Simply Christian* (HarperOne, 2006)

    o  Cited for his perspective on recognizing Jesus in the poor and joining in God's restorative mission through small acts of love.

2. Francis Chan, *Letters to the Church* (David C. Cook, 2018)

    o  Referenced for his critique of modern church systems that prioritize busyness over deep relational connection and community-building.

3. Christine Pohl, *Living into Community* (Eerdmans, 2012)

    o  Referenced for the idea that our presence when offered with love and humility, it becomes a powerful testimony of God's grace.

## Supporting Biblical References:

1. Isaiah 58:1–10 – God rebukes empty religious practices that ignore justice, mercy, and compassion, calling His people to worship through action.

2. Matthew 25:35–40 – Jesus links caring for "the least of these" with loving and serving Him directly.

3. Micah 6:8 – Summarizes God's desire for justice, mercy, and humility as essential to faithful living.

4. John 13:35 – Jesus identifies love as the distinguishing mark of true discipleship.

5. Galatians 6:2 – A call to carry one another's burdens as the fulfillment of Christ's law.

6. James 1:27 – Defines pure religion as caring for orphans and widows, connecting faith to compassionate action.

7. 1 Corinthians 12 – Describes the church as one body with many parts, each member playing a vital role in the community.

# CHAPTER 5 - OVERCOMING OBSTACLES TO AUTHENTIC CONNECTION

## Books Referenced:

1. John Mark Comer, *The Ruthless Elimination of Hurry* (WaterBrook, 2019)

    o Referenced to highlight how a fast-paced life hinders deep connection and love, reinforcing the need to slow down for authentic relationships.

2. R.T. Kendall, *Total Forgiveness* (Charisma House, 2007)

    o Quoted to describe the spiritual cost of unforgiveness and how releasing others opens the door to healing and growth.

3. Lewis B. Smedes, *Forgive and Forget: Healing the Hurts We Don't Deserve* (HarperOne, 2007)

    o Used to illustrate how forgiveness brings freedom and breaks the chains of bitterness.

4. Henry Cloud and John Townsend, *Boundaries* (Zondervan, 1992)

o   Referenced to encourage deeper, healthier connections by highlighting the need for honesty and emotional availability.

5.  Dietrich Bonhoeffer, *Life Together* (HarperOne, 1954)

    o   Quoted to challenge idealized visions of community and call readers to authentic, Christ-centered connection.

6.  Adam S. McHugh, *The Listening Life* (IVP Books, 2015)

    o   Used to explain listening as a spiritual discipline essential for connection, understanding, and empathy.

7.  Patrick Lencioni, *The Five Dysfunctions of a Team* (Jossey-Bass, 2002)

    o   Referenced to demonstrate how unresolved conflict erodes trust and how healthy confrontation strengthens unity.

## Supporting Biblical References:

1.  Matthew 5:23–24 – Teaches the urgency of reconciliation in maintaining both relational and spiritual health.

2.  Romans 12:10 – A call to love and honor one another, forming the basis for healthy, gospel-centered relationships.

3.  Matthew 18:15–17 – Outlines Jesus' approach to conflict resolution with humility and restoration.

4.  Philippians 2:3–5 – A model for humility and selflessness in community life.

5. Galatians 6:2 – Encourages believers to carry one another's burdens as an expression of Christ's law.

6. Job 2:11–13 – Shows the power of presence and silent support in times of grief.

7. John 4:1–26 – Demonstrates Jesus' willingness to break social and cultural barriers to connect with the Samaritan woman.

8. 1 Corinthians 12 – Emphasizes the interdependence of the church body and the unique role of each member.

9. John 13:34–35 – Declares that love is the defining mark of discipleship and true community.

## CHAPTER 6 – TRANSFORMATION THROUGH RELATIONSHIP

### Books Referenced:

1. Dallas Willard, *Renovation of the Heart* (NavPress, 2002)

    o Referenced for his foundational definition of spiritual formation as the internal transformation of character and will, highlighting the difference between outward activity and inward change.

2. John Wesley, *The Works of John Wesley, Volume 7: A Plain Account of Christian Perfection* (Abingdon Press, 1984)

    o Quoted to explain the Wesleyan view of discipleship and sanctification as a lifelong pursuit of holiness through grace and community.

3. Francis Chan, *Letters to the Church* (David C. Cook, 2018)

    o Cited to critique overly programmatic approaches to discipleship and to reinforce the relational, life-on-life model of mentoring and spiritual growth.

4. Henri Nouwen, *The Way of the Heart* (Ballantine Books, 1981)

    o Quoted to contrast the busyness of modern church life with the need for solitude, reflection, and being present with God.

5. James K.A. Smith, *You Are What You Love: The Spiritual Power of Habit* (Brazos Press, 2016)

    o Used to support the idea that our spiritual formation is shaped by repeated relational habits, not just knowledge or intention.

6. Dietrich Bonhoeffer, *Life Together* (HarperOne, 1954)

    o Referenced to describe the necessity of community for discipleship and the relational bond that forms when believers walk together through faith and struggle.

## Supporting Biblical References:

1. Matthew 4:19 – Jesus calls His disciples with a relational invitation to follow and be formed for purpose.

2. Romans 12:2 – Emphasizes the renewal of the mind as essential to spiritual transformation.

3. John 15:5 – Highlights the importance of abiding in Christ as the source of fruitfulness and spiritual growth.

4. Galatians 5:22-23 – Lists the fruit of the Spirit, pointing to the internal transformation discipleship should produce.

5. 2 Timothy 2:2 – Paul urges Timothy to pass on what he's learned in a generational model of discipleship.

6. Hebrews 10:24-25 – Encourages believers to spur one another on in love and not neglect gathering together.

7. Proverbs 27:17 – Illustrates how mutual relationships sharpen and strengthen our faith.

8. Matthew 18:15-17 – Provides a process for conflict resolution rooted in relationship and restoration.

9. Luke 10:38-42 – Shows the contrast between Martha's busyness and Mary's posture of presence with Jesus.

10. 2 Timothy 3:16 – Affirms the power of Scripture to teach, correct, and train us in righteousness.

## CHAPTER 7 - PRIORITIZING RELATIONAL LEADERSHIP

### Books Referenced:

1. Patrick Lencioni, *The Five Dysfunctions of a Team* (Jossey-Bass, 2002)

    o Referenced for exposing how a lack of trust and vulnerability undermines team health, aligning with the chapter's emphasis on relational integrity in leadership.

2. Brené Brown, *Daring Greatly* (Gotham Books, 2012)

- o   Quoted for insights on vulnerability and authenticity, emphasizing that true leadership is built on the courage to be real, not on image or control.

3. Carey Nieuwhof, *Didn't See It Coming* (WaterBrook, 2018)

- o   Cited for his analysis of the digital age's impact on connection, reinforcing the need for leaders to prioritize relational presence over curated content.

4. Paul Hersey, *The Situational Leader* (Warner Books, 1985)

- o   Referenced for supporting the call to adaptive leadership, especially when navigating diverse relational dynamics within a team or church body.

5. Francis Schaeffer, *The Great Evangelical Disaster* (Crossway Books, 1984)

- o   Cited for his critique of the church's drift toward structuralism, underscoring the need for relational integrity and gospel-centered authenticity.

6. James C. Hunter, *The World's Most Powerful Leadership Principle* (WaterBrook Press, 2004)

- o   Referenced for reinforcing servant leadership as the central model of influence and highlighting how love and humility shape lasting transformation.

## Supporting Biblical References:

1. Mark 10:51 – Jesus asks Bartimaeus what he wants, modeling leadership that listens first and assumes nothing.

2. Matthew 20:26-28 – Jesus defines true greatness through servant leadership, setting the standard for how leaders should serve.

3. 2 Corinthians 12:9-10 – Paul's openness about his weakness reflects the strength found in vulnerability, key to relational leadership.

4. 1 Timothy 1:2 & 2 Timothy 2:2 – Paul's relationship with Timothy exemplifies life-on-life investment and generational leadership.

## CHAPTER 8 - REDEFINING SUCCESS

### Books Referenced:

1. Eugene H. Peterson – *The Pastor: A Memoir* (HarperOne, 2011)

    o Quoted for his warning that performance-driven ministry is "a betrayal of the soul," offering a sobering reminder about the spiritual toll of chasing image over intimacy.

2. Francis Chan – *Letters to the Church* (David C Cook, 2018)

    o Referenced for his challenge to the modern church to resist flashiness and return to simple, faithful discipleship rooted in community.

3. Brené Brown – *Daring Greatly* (Avery, 2012)

    o Cited for insights on vulnerability and authenticity, especially in leadership contexts where trust is built through relational risk rather than perfection.

4. Carey Nieuwhof – *Didn't See It Coming* (WaterBrook, 2018)

    o   Cited for his discussion on emotional burnout and the dangers of equating success with platform or performance.

5. Charles Taylor – *A Secular Age* (Belknap Press, 2007)

    o   Referenced for his critique of cultural pressures toward control, speed, and efficiency, providing context for how these forces influence ministry values.

## Supporting Biblical References:

1. Matthew 25:35–40 – Jesus redefines success through acts of compassion and love, urging us to see Him in "the least of these."

2. 1 Corinthians 3:6 – Paul reminds the church that God, not human effort, is the source of true growth.

3. Matthew 5:3–12 – The Beatitudes reveal God's values, celebrating humility, mercy, and purity over worldly recognition.

4. Luke 15:10 – Heaven rejoices over one sinner who repents, revealing God's heart for transformation over performance.

5. Luke 5:16 – Jesus regularly withdrew to pray, modeling a rhythm of rest and intentional reflection amid the demands of ministry.

6. Judges 7 – God reduces Gideon's army to demonstrate that victory comes by His power, not numbers or human strength.

# CHAPTER 9 – SUSTAINING RELATIONAL CHURCH CULTURE

## Books Referenced:

1. Samuel Chand, *Cracking Your Church's Culture Code* (Jossey-Bass, 2011)

    o   Referenced for defining the power of church culture and identifying "cultural toxins" that hinder relational health and mission alignment.

2. Andy Stanley, *Deep and Wide* (Zondervan, 2012)

    o   Cited for the concept of creating "irresistible environments" that prioritize relational connection over performance or production.

3. Van Moody, *The People Factor* (Thomas Nelson, 2014)

    o   Referenced for exploring how relational dysfunction, trust, and emotional safety impact church health and unity.

4. Brené Brown, *Daring Greatly* (Gotham Books, 2012)

    o   Cited for insights on vulnerability, trust, and creating spaces where people feel safe enough to be honest and connected.

5. Patrick Lencioni, *The Advantage* (Jossey-Bass, 2012)

    o   Referenced for emphasizing trust, clarity, and shared purpose as essential components of a thriving, healthy organizational culture.

## Supporting Biblical References:

1. Matthew 5:16 – Encourages believers to live visibly impactful lives that glorify God through everyday acts of love and faithfulness.

2. Mark 6 – Describes Jesus sending out the disciples, showing a model of empowerment and relational partnership.

3. Luke 5:16 – Shows Jesus withdrawing to pray, modeling rest and reflection as vital for sustained ministry.

4. 1 Corinthians 3:6 – Paul clarifies that spiritual growth is God's work, not driven by human effort alone.

5. Matthew 25:35–40 – Provides a vision of true kingdom success rooted in compassion, service, and love.

# CHAPTER 10 - COMMUNITY BEYOND THE FOUR WALLS

## Books Referenced:

1. Henri Nouwen, *Life of the Beloved* (Crossroad, 2002)

    o Quoted for its reflections on human value, the call to love, and the importance of living out our belovedness in practical ways.

2. James K.A. Smith, *You Are What You Love* (Brazos Press, 2016)

    o Referenced for its insight into how practices shape desire and how relational discipleship forms lasting transformation.

## Supporting Biblical References:

1. Acts 2:44–47 – Describes the early church's radical generosity and the power of authentic, spirit-led community.

2. Acts 4:32 – Emphasizes the unity and shared heart among early believers.

3. 1 Corinthians 13:1–3 – Stresses that love is the essential ingredient for meaningful faith and service.

4. James 2:15–17 – Challenges believers to demonstrate their faith through action, not just words.

5. Matthew 22:39 – Reinforces the command to love others as we love ourselves.

6. John 13:34–35 – Jesus calls His disciples to be known by their love.

7. Micah 6:8 – Highlights God's call for justice, mercy, and humble living.

8. Galatians 6:2 – Calls believers to carry each other's burdens.

9. Romans 12:10 – Encourages devotion and honor in Christian community.

10. Ephesians 2:10 – Affirms that believers are created to do good works prepared by God.

11. 2 Timothy 1:7 – Reminds believers that God gives power, love, and self-discipline, not fear.

12. John 3:16 – Declares God's love in sending His Son, the foundation of the gospel message.

# **CONCLUSION**

## Books Referenced:

1. Dietrich Bonhoeffer, *Life Together* (HarperOne, 1954)

    o   Referenced for its deep insight into Christian community, shared spiritual life, and the sacred rhythm of living in unity.

2. Francis Chan, Letters *to the Church* (David C. Cook, 2018)

    o   Quoted for its passionate call to return to biblical community and to prioritize relational discipleship over religious routine.

## Supporting Biblical References:

1. Acts 2:42–47 – Describes the communal lifestyle and relational rhythm of the early church.

2. Romans 12:10 – Encourages deep, honoring relationships within the church family.

3. Ephesians 4:3–6 – Calls for Spirit-led unity and peace within the body of Christ.

4. Galatians 6:2 – Instructs believers to carry each other's burdens as an act of mutual care.

5. John 13:34–35 – Jesus' command to be known by love and connection, not just belief.

# EPILOGUE

## Supporting Biblical References:

1. Acts 4:32 – Depicts unity and generosity as hallmarks of early believers.

2. Micah 6:8 – Calls believers to walk humbly, act justly, and love mercy.

3. Galatians 6:2 – Reinforces shared burdens and practical love.

4. John 3:16 – Demonstrates the gospel's foundation: sacrificial love.

5. Matthew 5:14–16 – Reminds believers to be a light that brings visibility to the love of Christ.

# Acknowledgment Of Influence

Every word in this book came from a place of prayer, study, and real-life experience, but I know I didn't arrive here alone. No one's voice is formed in a vacuum. The thoughts shared throughout these pages have been shaped by so many others; pastors, mentors, teachers, and writers who helped me see things differently and love more fully.

Some of these ideas came to life during quiet moments with God. Others were stirred through books, conversations, and teachings that challenged me in the best kind of way. Even when their words aren't directly quoted, their influence runs quietly beneath the surface.

Writers like Dietrich Bonhoeffer, Francis Chan, Samuel Chand, and Patrick Lencioni have each played a part in how I think about the Church, leadership, and the culture we create. Their wisdom has helped me wrestle with truth and lean deeper into what it means to lead with love.

So to the voices that helped shape mine—thank you. Your work has mattered more than you may ever know.

www.ingramcontent.com/pod-product-compliance
Lightning Source LLC
Chambersburg PA
CBHW030448100526
44580CB00002B/28